BY ONE OF THE MOST
DECORATED AGENTS IN FBI HISTORY,
FORMER SPECIAL AGENT

JAMES A. MCGEE

The FCI Talladega Hostage Rescue

MOORSGATE
PRESS
NASHVILLE, TENNESSEE

MOORSGATE PRESS
5560 Franklin Pike Circle
Brentwood, Tennessee 37027

All rights reserved. No part of this publication may be reproduced, stored in retrieval system, or transmitted in any form or by any means, electronic, mechanical, photocopying, recording, or otherwise, without written permission of the publisher. For information regarding permission, write to:
Cold Tree Publishing, 5560 Franklin Pike Circle, Suite 112,
Brentwood, Tennessee 37027.
www.coldtreepublishing.com

Copyright © 2009 James A. McGee

Publisher's Cataloging-in-Publication data

McGee, James, A.
   Phase line green : The FCI Talladega hostage rescue / James A. McGee.
   p. cm.
   ISBN 978-0-98194-260-5
   ISBN 0-9819426-0-1
1. Hostages. 2. Rescues. 3. Federal Correctional Institution, Talladega, Alabama. 4. United States. Federal Bureau of Investigation. Hostage Rescue Team. I. Title.

HV6595 M4 2009
364.15421–dc22   2009923924

First Edition: May 2009
10 9 8 7 6 5 4 3 2 1

Moorsgate Press is an imprint of Cold Tree Publishng

Cover Design © 2009 Moorsgate Press
Cover and Interior Design by Bobby Dawson
Cover Photos: ©iStockphoto.com/clintspencer

Printed in Canada

*In memory of my father,
my brother,
and my grandfather.*

Subject: Praise

"A taut, gripping account of the FBI Hostage Rescue Team's brilliantly executed rescue of hostages held by ruthless Mariel Cubans at Talladega—the FBI at its best and a story well told by one of the team's assaulters."
— *Former U.S. Attorney General William Barr*

"Special Agent McGee offers the public a glimpse at the dedicated law enforcement officers who, without hesitation, risk their own lives to save the lives of others. The special agents who comprise the FBI HRT embody the spirit of fidelity, bravery, and integrity shared by all FBI agents. The HRT motto "Servare Vitas—To Save Lives" is testimony to this creed. There are many success stories that are often overlooked because nothing went wrong. The FCI Talladega Hostage Rescue is definitely one of these. This account captures the essence of law enforcement on the front lines. Every American needs to know who's guarding their freedoms and the sacrifice associated with performing this duty."
— *Former FBI Director William Sessions*

"Jim McGee is a national treasure, a genuine hero, and a shrewd observer of the human condition. *Phase Line Green* takes us through the breach point with raw honesty and rich detail. This is a man's book in a boy's world."
— *Andrew Lenchewski, Producer*

"*Phase Line Green*, a major contribution to the history of the FBI HRT, is written with an insider's knowledge of a true-life event about real FBI agents."
— *Don Zembiec, Special Agent FBI (retired)*

"Jim McGee has captured the essence of being on the front lines of a national counterterrorism team. His description of the day-to-day realities and preparation that go into a successful hostage rescue are detailed throughout this gripping text. All the elements are here—from the serious to the lighter side. This is a must read for anyone interested in what it is like to be a part of the "tip of the spear."
—*David S. Corderman, PhD, Former Member*
FBI Hostage Rescue Team

Subject: Table of Contents

Preface	xi
Part 1 Rite of Passage	1
Chapter 1 Red Mist	3
Chapter 2 Train Like You Fight, and Fight Like You Train	17
Chapter 3 Honing the Edge	29
Chapter 4 When the Balloon Goes Up	51
Part 2 Stand By, Stand By	69
Chapter 5 Hurry Up and Wait	71
Chapter 6 Prep Time	95
Chapter 7 Showtime	121
Chapter 8 French Toast for Breakfast	139
Part 3 Quiet Professionals	163
Chapter 9 Hi Honey, I'm Home!	167
Chapter 10 Servare Vitas	181
Epilogue	195
Author's Note	203
Acknowledgments	205
Endnotes	207

Subject: Preface

Within each of us, we harbor a lifetime of memories. Some of these memories haunt our dreams, finding refuge in our subconscious. My sleep is chronically disturbed by memories of tragic, life-or-death incidents and the feelings of helplessness that come with the news of unexpected death. Sensing anguished cries of despair, I awake to find that they are my own. Recognizing these recollections and reducing them to writing is the mechanism I've chosen to facilitate their escape from my nighttime thoughts.

Within society, there are those who choose to save lives by risking their own and in turn reduce the consequences of tragic events. It is my intent to memorialize and remind readers of such heroic actions, specifically the FCI Talladega hostage rescue.

I have striven to base my interpretations on my training, my personal experiences, and my firsthand involvement in the various events described within this text. I am keenly aware of the various sensitivities associated with hostage rescue and counterterrorism operations and I have not compromised any tactics or revealed any trade secrets. The names of individuals have been included only with their permission or if available to the public through open source information.

As a career law enforcement officer, I have prepared reams of reports, which would potentially be subjected to courtroom scrutiny; therefore, I have always written in a style that includes "Just the facts, ma'am." My comments are candid and my own, leaving little gray area in between. Hopefully, for the reader, this results in a behind-the-scenes glimpse into the counterterrorism operator's world. A world seemingly encapsulated by violence, but truly focused on the preservation of freedom.

What follows is based on my perspective of events as they transpired. The views expressed are neither endorsed nor necessarily the opinion of the FBI.

Duty is Ours; consequences are God's.
—General Stonewall Jackson, CSA

PHASE LINE GREEN

File No.: Part One
Subject: Rite of Passage

Deploying to an incident like the 1991 FCI Talladega hostage crisis requires more than the average SWAT team. Missions of this type require the expertise of a specialized full-time civilian counterterrorist team. Only one team exists in the United States to fulfill this role and that is the FBI Hostage Rescue Team (HRT).

File No.: Chapter One
Subject: Red Mist

I do believe in destiny. Although I didn't know it at the time, until March 16, 1990, my life had been spent preparing for the events that would transpire from that point on.

I entered on duty with the FBI on November 17, 1986, and I was now coming up on my four-year anniversary as a special agent. I took a seat outside the office of the assistant special agent in charge (ASAC) of the Albuquerque Field Division and waited for my appointment with him to discuss career options. As I sat there, I took the time to reflect.

My experiences as an agent over the last four years had been about what I expected. As a former Deputy Sheriff for the Ventura County Sheriff's Office (VCSO) in Southern California, the transition to agent life had come easy. I had viewed my new role as a fed as more or less synonymous with the plainclothes special enforcement details[1] we had had with the sheriff's office.

In March 1987, as a new agent with a prior law enforcement background, I had been thrust into investigating criminal violations known as reactive. The Reactive Squad in the Albuquerque Field Division of the FBI, my first office of assignment, addressed fugitive, kidnapping, and bank robbery investigations as well as Domestic Police Cooperation Matters, which is *bureauese* for any other criminal act that local law enforcement needed some assistance with. My training agent, a senior special agent whose job was to show me the ropes, was a hard-nosed, no-nonsense, former New York agent named Don Zembiec. Don was the Albuquerque FBI SWAT Team Leader and the type of individual who I knew, from the moment I met him, would be there when the proverbial shit hit the fan.

My first contact with Don had been in January 1987 at the FBI Academy in Quantico, Virginia. I was an agent trainee completing my required coursework. One day, between classes, I noticed an ominous-looking individual standing outside one of the adjoining classrooms. He stood about six foot four and was dressed in a gray pinstriped suit and the requisite black Florsheim wing tip shoes that stereotype a G-man. He was "holding court" with several very attentive listeners. I moved in closer so I could hear the conversation. The man was describing the tedious preparations he systematically followed as he zeroed in on a target with his .308-caliber rifle. He emphasized the necessity of a smooth, unanticipated trigger pull coupled with an unobstructed sight alignment. His concluding comment, "I love to see the red mist," ended the conversation. He made this comment as a matter of fact. No emotion. His tone of voice didn't change. This was how he measured success. Was this guy a government assassin?

By March 1987, after sixteen weeks of New Agent Training classes, I was ready to hit the ground running when I arrived in the Albuquerque Division. Much to my surprise (and satisfaction), when I was formally introduced to my training agent, Don Zembiec, or "Z-man" for short, I immediately recognized him as none other than the ominous-looking guy I'd overheard at the Academy.

I'll never forget walking down to the garage with Don on that first day in the Albuquerque office. As we approached his FBI-assigned car or, as Don referred to it, his "Bu-steed," I noticed a bullet hole in the right front fender of his blue-over-white, four-door Chevy Caprice. Upon noticing my fixation with the wound his BU-steed had sustained, he nonchalantly stated, "Yeah, I took a round while doing a neighborhood investigation. No big deal. The guy waited until I was across the street knocking on the neighbor's front door to shoot my car. Besides, the guy I was looking for wasn't even in the area. The shooter was just paranoid."

Some time later, I asked Don about his "red mist" comment. He confided in me that he had been talking about prairie dogs. Apparently, prairie dogs make for great target practice when out on the mesas surrounding Albuquerque.

Albuquerque, New Mexico, is located adjacent to the Rocky Mountains, near the lumbar vertebrae of this jagged north-south spine that extends the length of the continent. Coincidently, I was born in Albuquerque, and I can remember frequently being asked to describe the geographic location of the nation's forty-seventh state. The population of New Mexico is approximately one million people, with over half of these residents living in the Albuquerque metropolitan area. The city is a mixture of cultures: Anglo, Hispanic, and American Indian. It is also the crossroads for Interstate 40, which runs east and west, and Interstate 25, which runs north and south. The crossroads combined with the reasonably mild climate creates a suitable environment for a large transient population. From 1987 to 1990, Don and I shagged a lot of leads together. Many times we included Carl, another agent who had been in my New Agents' class and had also been sent to Albuquerque for his first office of assignment.

One Friday afternoon in the fall of 1989, I fielded a telephone call in the Albuquerque office from an agent out of the Denver Division. The Denver agent told me he had a federal fugitive warrant for an individual identified as Gregory Dewey Clifford. Clifford was wanted for the mutilation homicide of his estranged wife. Clifford was suspected of stabbing his wife to death. In an effort to hide her body, he stuffed her remains into a cardboard box. But he couldn't get her body to fit into the box—so he hacked off her arms and legs. He stuffed the dismembered limbs into the box alongside the torso. Apparently, he had left the now-closed box sitting in her second-story apartment. It was winter at the time and the heater was on in the apartment. The first-floor tenants became suspicious when they noticed something dripping from a wet spot on their ceiling. The apartment heater coupled with normal decomposition had liquefied the body.

Now Clifford had crossed the Colorado state line into New Mexico and was suspected of being in Albuquerque. The Denver agent told me Clifford was expecting a money order to be wired to him at a local Albuquerque bank on the following Monday. Apprehending Clifford would be as easy as staking out the bank on Monday morning and picking him up when he arrived to get his money order. That's what the Denver agent thought. I wasn't so sure. A lot could happen over the weekend to spook this guy. I got up from my desk and walked across the "bullpen." In the late eighties, the bullpen was a large room where the (mostly male) agents who worked Reactive Crimes sat and shared information. The desks all butted up against each other. There were no computers, just rotary phones and a couple of electric typewriters. I found Carl and explained what I had.

Since Clifford was known to be transient, I suggested we take a drive down Broadway and look around the flophouses. Carl agreed. We drove past the Salvation Army and a couple of other soup kitchens that lined northwest Broadway. As we passed a Disabled American Veterans (DAV) hall located on the west side of Broadway, I made a quick left into the parking lot.

"What are you doing?" Carl asked.

"I want to take another look at Clifford's NCIC printout." I was referring to the teletype printout from the National Criminal Information

Center. Connected end-to-end and folded like an accordion, the printout provided copious information about the federal fugitive warrant. As I riffled through countless pages of information about Clifford's past criminal history and his physical description, I found what I was looking for: the category that describes known scars and tattoos. Turns out, Clifford was known to have a tattoo on his right forearm that bore the motto Death Before Dishonor. I knew this was a military tattoo common among airborne troops.

"Look at this," I said to Carl, gesturing toward the printout. "Clifford is inside that DAV hall sitting at the bar having a beer. I'll bet you I'm right." There was only one way to see if my gut feeling was correct. Carl and I both agreed we needed to go inside the hall and have a look around. We got out of the car and approached the front door of the hall. We each carried our bureau-issued Smith & Wesson model 13 .357-caliber wheel gun in a waist holster. Opposite the side where the gun was holstered, we each had a speed loader pouch with six more rounds. Positioned on our lower backs, tucked into the waistband of our pants, we both had a set of handcuffs. Our gear was positioned just like we'd been shown at the FBI Academy and we were dressed in Standard Academy Attire: J. Edgar Hoover white dress shirt, dark necktie, and sport coat.

Carl was a solid agent. He didn't shy away from confrontation. I knew what his capabilities were, but Carl didn't have any prior law enforcement experience, and I knew this situation was probably the diciest he'd ever faced. Still, we had been through New Agents' class together; he was one of the best shots in the class, and I never saw him get flustered during classroom arrest scenarios. But then again, this wasn't the classroom anymore.

We decided we would enter the hall, move to the bar, and order a drink. After our eyes adjusted to the dark, we would "casually" look around to see if Clifford was seated anywhere. I entered the hall first and moved straight ahead toward the bar with Carl right behind me. We weaved around several small tables where a handful of customers were seated. Smoke and a lack of ambient light kept the room dark, resulting in low visibility for us. A jukebox was playing some indiscernible country song. The volume was low.

As I reached the bar, Carl took a position immediately to my left. I leaned forward and glanced to my right, taking a brief look at the faces of two other men seated at the bar. The first guy was a heavyset older white male. Not Clifford. He looked at me and I nodded. The second guy was looking straight ahead. I could see his profile. He slowly turned in my direction. He had long black hair pulled back into a ponytail and was wearing a standard military-issued olive drab field jacket. He was an American Indian with a heavily pocked face. Gregory Dewey Clifford. I waited for Clifford to look away then I slowly reached over to Carl and motioned for him to look down the bar past me. As he looked I said, "He's gonna make us in these suits." We stood out like two sore thumbs.

"What'll it be?" said the bartender before we could react.

"Two Buds," I said.

"Are you guys veterans?" the bartender said surveying our coats and ties.

"No, but my dad is a New Mexico veteran, and he recommended we come by here for a beer. Maybe you know him—John McGee." The part about my dad being a New Mexico veteran was true; the rest was pure BS.

To my surprise, the guy seated to my right chimed in and said, "Yeah, I know John McGee."

I couldn't believe it. I watched Clifford as he sipped on a drink and listened to our conversation.

Before I could say anything else, the bartender said, "Sorry guys, you gotta be a veteran to get served."

"No problem," I said. "Rules are rules." I shook the hand of the guy who said he knew John McGee, and Carl and I went out the front door back into the parking lot.

Dusk was quickly approaching. I checked my watch. It was after 5:00 p.m. I knew most of the agents were already heading home for the weekend. I told Carl that we'd need to get some backup and that I'd get on the radio to see who was available. While Carl watched the front door of the bar, I got into the car and reached out over the bureau radio for any agent on the air who could respond to assist. Within seconds, I received a response.

"This is Number Three, SA McGee, what's your location?" At first, I hesitated to answer. "Number Three" was my new squad supervisor, Supervisory Special Agent (SSA) Lee Teitsworth. He was brand-new to the Albuquerque Division, straight from FBI Headquarters in Washington DC. He seemed like a good guy, not the typical empty suit. I guess we'd find out how he performed on the streets.

"Yes sir, Number Three," I responded. "I'm at the DAV hall located on Broadway NW. You'll see us parked in the side parking lot. Do you have an ETA?"

"About five minutes. I'm just pulling out of the office."

I didn't receive any other responses over the radio. Federal Friday is the same everywhere…even in the FBI.

While Carl and I waited for SSA Teitsworth to arrive, I said to Carl, "We're going to need some uniform presence." We needed a couple of local Albuquerque Police Department (APD) street cops to assist. Having a couple of cops in uniform would reduce the chance for resistance from the other patrons when we reentered the bar. This was a high-crime area, and, therefore, heavily patrolled. I got out of the car and stood looking south down Broadway. Sure enough, a marked APD patrol car came around the corner. I flagged the unit over, flashed my FBI credentials and asked the patrol officer if he'd like to help arrest a mutilation murderer. I knew what his response would be. As a beat cop, it's not often you're flagged down by the FBI and asked to help arrest a violent felon. This officer was young, and probably had less than a year out of the Albuquerque Police Academy. He immediately agreed to assist, and pulled his Blue-and-White around next to my car. I briefly described the situation and asked him to call for another marked unit. I had a plan in mind. I pulled Carl aside and began to explain.

SSA Teitsworth arrived on scene first. A few minutes later, the second marked unit showed up. No one had entered or exited the front door of the bar since Carl and me. I knew there was a back door, but anyone going in or coming out that way would have had to pass by the side of the building where we were positioned. Carl continued to watch the front door. He already knew what I had in mind. SSA Teitsworth, the two APD officers, and I gathered around the front of my car.

"What's your plan, Jim?" said SSA Teitsworth.

I could see Carl glancing over at me. I pulled a blank three-by-five index card out of my jacket pocket and quickly sketched the floor plan of the inside of the bar as I explained. "Boss, Clifford was sitting at the bar, to the far right as you enter the building. He seemed pretty wasted. I doubt he's moved.

"I'd like for you to go in first, move straight across the room and take a position by the back door. That will keep him from running.

"As soon as you enter, I'll give you to the count of ten to get to the back door. Then we're coming in. I'll be first, followed by Carl. The two APD officers will be right behind us.

"They'll be armed with their standard Remington 870 shotguns. (I knew both officers had shotguns mounted to the front dash of their patrol cars. This is standard issue for most PDs.) Carl and I will move directly toward Clifford with our guns drawn. The two APD officers will break right and left after they enter the room.

"Oh, yeah, as the APD guys enter, I want them to rack a round into their shotguns. I think we all know what an attention getter that is."

In essence, I had provided SSA Teitsworth with an arrest plan in the format of a five-paragraph operations order. I had touched on each requirement, best remembered by the acronym SMEAC, which stands for Situation, Mission, Execution, Administrative/Logistics, and Command/Control.

SSA Teitsworth was quiet for a second, and then said, "Sounds good, let's do it."

We all went to the trunks of our cars and pulled out our individual soft body armor and put it on over our white dress shirts. I ditched my sport coat and put on my bureau blue raid jacket with the eight-inch, gold-colored, block letters *FBI* stenciled across the back. The two cops already had body armor on under their uniform shirts. Each cop retrieved his shotgun, cleared the weapon, and then assembly loaded five rounds into the ammunition tube to make sure a round wasn't prematurely chambered. We didn't need a weapons jam as we entered the bar and racked a round into the shotguns. That could happen if they tried to chamber one round on top of another. I checked and made sure my revolver was loaded. I also pulled out my cuffs and worked them to make sure they hadn't double locked on me by accident. This happened occasionally if the cuffs got bumped, and it really disrupted the flow of an arrest if you had to stop, retrieve a cuff key, and unlock your cuffs before you could put them on the crook.

The five of us moved up to the front door of the DAV hall. I gave SSA Teitsworth the thumbs-up and said, "Ten seconds." He nodded at me, put his hand on the bar door, then pushed it open and entered. I started counting out loud, "One, two, three, four, five (nothing sounded unusual from inside), six, seven, eight (I leaned my body into the door), nine, ten…let's go." I pushed through the door. Again, the room was dark and hazy. My eyes had to adjust. As I moved through the tables to where Clifford had been sitting, I announced, "FBI, everyone get your hands in the air." I could see Clifford now; he wasn't moving. No sign of SSA Teitsworth; he must have been out of sight behind the bar by the back door. Everyone in the bar just looked at me dumbfounded. That all changed the minute the APD officers racked their shotguns. As predicted, hands *flew* into the air upon hearing this universal and unmistakable sound.

Clifford hadn't even turned around when I reached him. I holstered my gun and pushed him off his barstool so he was leaning over the bar. Carl was covering me. I said, "Gregory Dewey Clifford, I'm with the FBI and we have a warrant for your arrest." He said nothing. I told him to put his hands behind his back. He complied, and I cuffed him. I did a quick pat down for weapons. He was clean. I grabbed him by the back of his collar and the chain that links the handcuffs and turned him toward the door. SSA Teitsworth was in front of me now, clearing the way to the front door. We emptied into the parking lot. The APD officers came out last. As we moved toward one of the marked APD units, Clifford looked at me and said, "You owe me for RESMUR."[2] I didn't know what he was talking about. He said it again.

I turned to SSA Teitsworth and asked him if he knew what Clifford was talking about.

"I think he's talking about the murder of two FBI agents, Jack

Coler and Ron Williams, in 1975 at the Pine Ridge Indian Reservation in South Dakota. One of the shooters was a scumbag named Leonard Peltier. He's doing life."

Since APD was with us on the arrest, Clifford was booked into the Bernalillo county jail. Normally we took all arrestees to the federal lockup in Los Lunas, New Mexico. Clifford was extradited back to Colorado to face the murder charge and, ultimately, was convicted and sentenced to life in prison. The State of Colorado offers the death sentence but it is rarely administered. Clifford would have been a good candidate. As far as his involvement in RESMUR, I found out he did assist with corroborating the case against Leonard Peltier and was subsequently entered into the witness protection program. He later left the program and resumed his life of crime. This all happened long before we encountered him in Albuquerque.

In early December 1989, not long after the Clifford arrest, an airtel (this was the standard bureau hardcopy communication in those days for passing information between field divisions and FBIHQ) was disseminated to all SAs. This airtel announced the upcoming selection that would be conducted in March 1990 for any agent interested in joining the Hostage Rescue Team (HRT). I'd heard this same announcement the year before, but had opted to work the streets a year longer to gain more experience. Now, with four years of experience under my belt, I had demonstrated my investigative and tactical skills by locating and arresting a number of violent federal fugitives like Clifford. This year I wanted to give selection a shot.

So here I sat, holding the airtel and its attached questionnaire, waiting to go into the office of Assistant Special Agent in Charge (ASAC) Teitsworth. Since the arrest of Clifford, Lee Teitsworth had been promoted to the number two agent in the Albuquerque

Division. We were also on a first-name basis now. I heard him hang up the phone. His office door was open and he was seated at his desk. He turned around and said, "Come in, Jim. What's up?"

"Lee, remember last year when I talked about attending the HRT selection?"

He took off his reading glasses and said, "Yes."

"Well, there's another selection this March. I'd like to give it a shot this time."

Lee looked at me and said, "If you do this, it will screw up your chances to move up in this outfit. Do you realize that?" I thought about Lee's comment. At the time, I didn't understand how belonging to an elite counterterrorist team could have a negative impact on your long-term career advancement within the FBI. Years later, I realized the management ranks of the FBI primarily consist of professional bureaucrats who achieve advancement through backdoor politics and face time. An outfit like the HRT, which selects members based on performance, is a threat to those who rely upon political posturing to get ahead.

"Lee," I said, "was the HRT around when you were at my stage in the bureau?" I knew Lee was an old SWAT guy from the San Francisco Division.

"No."

"If it had been, would you have tried out?"

Lee looked directly into my eyes and smiled. "Yes, Jim, I would have."

Lee Teitsworth was the exception to the rule when it came to management. He was honest and he didn't hold punches. That was all I needed to hear. Lee gave me his blessing and full support. He said he would talk to the special agent in charge (SAC) to get his approval.

At that moment I knew my life would never be the same again.

Beginning New Year's Day of 1990, I intensified my workouts. I knew, from talking to guys who had tried to make the HRT in the past, that the two-week selection course was brutally tough. Physically, I felt I was in good shape. I knew I would need to increase my cardiovascular capacity, find a pool and start swimming, and spend more time at the shooting range.

Preparing for something like the HRT selection course all boils down to what your personal level of intensity is when you train. Some people work out to keep off the pounds; others merely go through the motions and use their time at the gym as a social event. A small percentage of people train with an objective, a *focus*. These individuals always start the stopwatch before every run and try to beat their previous time. They always add a few more pounds to the bar and strive for a new personal best. Training with this type of intensity raises your personal threshold for pain, and as a result, you continue when others stop. I was intimately familiar with this mind-set. As a former NCAA Division I running back, I had trained and competed against the greatest athletes in the world. As a competitive power lifter, I had pushed my body to the absolute extreme in the gym where my workouts frequently included 600-pound full squats, 600-pound dead lifts, and 435-pound bench presses. At five foot eleven and 210 pounds, I was able to rep out forty strict pull-ups, cover forty yards in 4.6 seconds and run a mile in under five minutes. My combination of strength, speed, and endurance would work to my advantage. I knew that over the course of the two-week selection process, fatigue would set in. Those in the best condition were the least likely to suffer an injury through fatigue.

I started routinely running the La Luz Trail up the western face of the Sandia Mountains in Albuquerque with Don Zembiec's teenaged son, Douglas. This thirteen-mile run had a 5,500-foot elevation at the base that increased to over 12,000 feet at the top. I backed off my heavy weight lifting and increased my push-ups, pull-ups and sit-ups. I did "grinders" to incorporate push-ups and sit-ups into my runs: you stop every two minutes during a six-mile run and do a set of each. Each time you stop, the number of repetitions increases by five. By the time you reach the last set you're over one hundred reps for each exercise. This physical regimen, coupled with several visits to the firing range per week would prepare me for HRT selection in the tangible and/or measurable areas. The other more intrinsic characteristics included initiative, perseverance, judgment, compatibility, trainability, discipline, loyalty, leadership, maturity, and other qualities that cannot be quantitatively measured or altered through training.

After ten weeks of intense preparation, I departed Albuquerque for the FBI Academy at Quantico, Virginia, on March 16, 1990, to attend the HRT selection. Physically and mentally, I knew I was ready. The techniques I utilized to prepare myself mentally for this challenge were the same ones I employed to prepare for any competition: I envisioned success. Prior to now, my life experiences and choices seemed without direction, like an unfamiliar road leading to an unknown destination. Suddenly it all fell into place. I knew my destiny and it was within my grasp. I had one goal in mind. *Failure was not an option.*

File No.: Chapter Two
Subject: Train Like You Fight, and Fight Like You Train

"Hotel at green," whispered the Hotel Team Leader (TL) into the small, push-to-talk microphone that was externally secured to the front left shoulder of his load-bearing vest. "Hotel TL, this is Alpha One," came the response. "I copy… Hotel at green."

As the number one man in the line of march, I was running point. I transfixed my MP5A3 fully automatic submachine gun on the front door of the crisis site. I focused my gaze on my designated field of fire with absolute concentration. I couldn't even allow myself to blink. Action versus reaction is a proven fact. If the door opened suddenly, I had to be ready to respond instinctively. In the event of compromise, hostages could be killed. From beneath my black assault helmet, sweat rolled down my forehead and collected on my Neanderthal (as my wife calls it) brow before falling to the ground. Immediately behind my position were seven other operators who were poised to move when I moved. When the number two man in the line of march had ensured that I was in position and "off safe," he gave the thumbs-up to the rest of the assault team. Once the number eight man, tail-end Charlie, received the thumbs-up, he reached forward with his weak hand and gently squeezed the arm of the operator immediately in front of him. This process continued until number two received a "squeeze-back." The TL then advised Alpha One, the on-scene commander (OSC) for the operation, of Hotel's status at *phase line green*. This is the final position before an assault commences; in most cases, this position is the breach point. Three other assault teams, Golf, Echo, and Charlie, were positioned at their designated entry points. All three teams advised they were at green.

We would access the crisis site through four different breach points. Hotel, Golf, and Echo teams would each enter through one of three external doors. Charlie team would enter through the external cinder block wall of the structure. The assault team breachers were responsible for setting up and firing the charge at their team's designated entry point. Each breacher, the number four man in the line of march, would adhere a linear shaped charge, consisting primarily of C-4 plastic explosives,[3] inserted into a channel cut from one side of a sheet of EPIFOAM (similar to Styrofoam), to the designated entry point. Once the C-4 was in place, they attached a pre-measured roll of non-electric (NONEL) shock tube[4] to it. Next, they unwound the shock tube and tied the loose end into a shooter, which they would fire upon command.

In addition to the four assault teams, there were four two-man sniper/observer (S/O) teams positioned at four locations around the crisis site. Each S/O team had been in their respective location for various lengths of time gathering intelligence about the crisis site and the occupants within. The S/Os were now tasked with covering the movement of the four assault teams from phase line yellow, the last point of cover and concealment, to phase line green. The S/Os would "jack-rabbit," or change radio frequencies, from the sniper net to the assault net so they could monitor our communications.

I continued to focus on the front door. I watched for any movement of the doorknob. I listened for any noise from the other side of the door. The Operations Order (OPORD), issued just before the operation commenced, indicated that at least six heavily armed terrorists (tangos) were holding two hostages inside the 10,000-square-foot structure. The hostages included an American ambassador and his wife. Each member of the assault force had studied floor plans of the crisis site provided during the briefing. The entire assault should take about a minute based on the known square footage of the building. Delays would occur only if the assault teams were met with significant resistance. All four assault teams would move concurrently, the overall objective being to rescue the hostages.

Upon the Execute command, my directions were explicit and predetermined. I would enter the exterior door of the living room while simultaneously engaging and neutralizing any threat. I would then turn left and "run the long wall." My route would end in the back left corner on the opposite side of the living room. I would hold my position until the TL designated the living room as clear. This plan sounded great and functioned like clockwork during rehearsals, but Murphy (If it can go wrong, it will) always showed up when you least expected him.

I stood motionless outside the front door of the crisis site. My MP5 was tucked into my right shoulder. I was careful not to rub the exterior wall of the crisis site with my right elbow and end up compromising our presence by alerting the terrorists inside the building. I heard Alpha One through my earpiece. "All elements are at green, stand by... stand by. TLs you have compromise authority.[5] I have control. Five... four...three...two (the snipers engaged targets-of-opportunity)...one (the explosive breaches were detonated), execute...execute!"

Alpha One's Execute command was given, but, as the number one man, it was all but lost in the thunderous noise made by the explosive breach. I immediately moved through the gaping hole in the solid-core wood door and entered the rectangular-shaped living room. The room was full of smoke and dust from the blast, and visibility was limited. I briefly contemplated whether to don my gasmask. This was the TL's call. As I moved, I yelled, "Get down, get down!" My command was intended to direct anyone in the living room to drop to the floor, and not following it significantly increased their chances of getting shot. I immediately turned the business end of my MP5 to the left and began my deliberate but hasty movement along my predesignated route. As the first man into the crisis site, my initial concern is always the corners of a room. Entering behind an explosive breach or a flash-bang virtually guarantees that any threat located in the center of the room is neutralized. The shrapnel coming off a solid-core wood door coupled with the overpressure from the blast is deadly. "Never enter a room without a boom" is a good rule to follow.

I reached the front left corner of the living room and turned to the right; my field of fire was now directed toward the back left corner of the living room. I continued to move along my predesignated route. Discipline is fundamental to close quarter battle (CQB).[6] Discipline combined with confidence in your teammates. I knew that any threat outside my field of fire would be addressed accordingly. You *can't* panic. You *can't* get a case of happy feet and deviate from your predetermined route. You *do* have to think on your feet and make split-second decisions that will very likely determine if someone lives or dies.

I reached the back left corner of the living room and again turned to my right. This is the point at which my predetermined movement stopped. My field of fire now shifted to the back right corner of the living room, about ten meters downrange. Through the gray dust I could see a man holding a weapon. I knew no operator would be at this location. Target identification is one of the first principles when engaging a potential threat. The weapon looked like a wheel gun, a .357 Smith & Wesson K-Frame revolver. I continued to yell, "Get down, get down!" as I ran my route. Here was a case of non-compliance. I yelled, "Tango, tango!" as a warning to the other operators. After identification, target acquisition is the next principle when engaging a threat. As the front post lined up with the rear aperture of my MP5, I began to pull slack on the trigger. Trigger pull and shot placement are the next principles. The adage "Smooth is Fast" ensures that a) you don't jerk the trigger and b) you place the rounds into an area that will incur the most physical trauma. Vital organs are key; a shot to the brain will cause the most trauma. I fired two successive rounds. The tango went down behind a couch.

During the briefing, the S/Os had informed us that the living room was a potential hot spot. Their intelligence was accurate; a person who met the physical description of one of the hostages was seated on the couch. I held my position, and yelled, "Danger area, danger area!" From my position, I didn't have a clear view of what was behind the couch where the tango had collapsed. This area needed to be approached cautiously and the status of the tango needed to be confirmed immediately.

When I initially entered the living room and went left, the number two man followed me through the breach and turned right. His predetermined route would take him to the front right corner of the living room. He would clear this corner and turn to his left. His field of fire at this point would be the back right corner of the living room. The number two man and I would have overlapping fields of fire. The number three man in the line of march is the TL. He and the number four man, the breacher, would fill the middle of the living room. Number four focused on a closed door in the middle of the back wall. The floor plans indicated that this door led to an adjoining family room. The number five man moved in behind number two and covered a closed door in the front right corner, which led into an adjacent bedroom. Once number five had his gun on the closed door, number two yelled, "Moving forward!" He then quickly moved forward to check the danger area behind the couch. Number two checked and confirmed the tango had met his demise. Apparently, number two had also engaged the tango from his position in the front right corner of the living room.

"Clear!" announced number two. "Clear!" I yelled, echoing number two. With this information, the TL yelled, "Hotel, clear!" to both ensure that numbers six, seven, and eight didn't inadvertently enter the living room and cross someone's field of fire and to give them the go ahead to enter the living room. Immediately, numbers six, seven, and eight in the line of march entered. This tactic is called a safety clear and relies on good communication and a thorough understanding of individual and assault team assignments by all.

Number six rapidly crossed the living room toward the couch where the hostage was seated. He grabbed him by an arm, performed a cursory search for weapons, and, as the Standard Operating Procedure (SOP) requires, cuffed the hostage's hands behind his back with flex-cuffs. To *assume* the hostage is a friendly can easily result in making an *ass* out of *you* and *me* if the Stockholm Syndrome[7] has taken effect. Number six then escorted the hostage out of the living room back through the initial breach point. Once outside the crisis site, the team paramedic examined the hostage to survey his physical status. The hostage was then loaded into a waiting Hughes 540 Little Bird helicopter, which had landed during the assault in a grass-covered landing zone (LZ) approximately thirty meters from the crisis site. Once all the hostages were extracted, the Little Bird was sitting there, rotor turning, for the purpose of expeditiously airlifting the hostages away from the crisis site.

Concurrent with successfully removing the hostage from the crisis site, the Hotel team members stacked behind numbers four and five who continued to cover their respective doors. One operator would stay behind and guard the dead tango. We conducted entry through the doors into the adjacent family room and bedroom simultaneously. Now number four and number five were on point and would be the first into their respective rooms. I was behind number four. Dave Corderman, who had entered the living room as number seven, was behind number five. Dave, a seasoned operator and former Marine, could do it all. The quintessential operator, Dave was a trained sniper, lead climber, swimmer, and an excellent shot. Dave and I each reached around our point man and checked our respective doors to see if they were locked. Mine wasn't, Dave's was. I pulled a flash-bang off the back of my point man's tactical vest and pulled the pin. Careful not to release the spoon on the flash-bang, I reached back around, turned the doorknob with my free hand, and then shoved the family room door open. I lobbed the flash-bang into the family room. One and a half seconds later, a concussion equivalent to one-quarter stick of dynamite rocked the family room. We entered immediately after the concussion.

Confronted with a locked bedroom door, Dave called out, "Breacher up!" This signaled number eight, the secondary Hotel team breacher, to move over to the bedroom door and shotgun the lock. This was successfully accomplished with two ceramic shotgun rounds strategically fired from a sawed-off, pistol grip Remington 870 shotgun that all breachers carry slung over their shoulders. Once number eight successfully breached the bedroom door, Dave lobbed a flash-bang into the room and waited for the concussion. One and a half seconds later, Bang! Dave and company were in.

The rooms that Dave and I had just entered completed Hotel team's initial responsibilities pursuant to the OPORD. The other three assault teams were handling all other interior areas. As number four and I entered the family room, number four turned left. "Reading" his movement, I turned right. Since there was no right—a wall was there—I continued straight ahead. Number four had chosen to go left because, unless the movement is predetermined, an assault team member always goes to the threat. Because number four had determined that there was nothing immediately present straight ahead, he turned to the left and toward the unknown. All operators must possess the ability to read the threat immediately upon entering a room, make a decision, and act accordingly. Even if the decision is wrong, we must make one. Otherwise, the flow of the assault is disrupted. This tactic goes by a couple of names: "light, heavy," heavy being the threat, or "SAS." This refers to the British Special Air Service, who are considered the true plank owners[8] when it comes to counterterrorist teams and innovators of CQB tactics.

From where I stood, I could hear Dave getting some trigger time in the adjacent bedroom. He must have run into some unfriendlys. Our room was clear of any tangos or hostages so far. I continued to move forward along the wall. The family room was L-shaped. Basically, we had entered at the top of the *L*. The room configuration doglegged right. At the corner where the room turned, I paused. The TL also entered the room and lined up behind me on the wall. Hotel's TL, J.D., was a highly respected operator whom I admired. He was a battle-hardened former Marine and Vietnam vet with the scars to show it. J.D. was in his eighth year as a "shooter," which far exceeded the four-year norm.

J.D. pulled a flash-bang off the back of my vest. I held point at the corner of the *L*. J.D. pulled the pin on the flash-bang and lobbed it around the corner. As soon as I heard the concussion, I moved straight ahead. I walked hastily with my knees bent, my assault boots striking the floor heel-to-toe to reduce disruption of my sight picture, thus allowing me to shoot on the move. J.D. looped the corner right behind me. I heard him yell, "Tango, tango!" I heard the distinct action of his MP5 as he unloaded a burst of rounds into the tango. My route didn't deviate. I reached the bottom of the *L*, the back wall of the structure. I turned right to extend my field of fire across to where J.D. had engaged the tango. I knew that J.D. had placed, with surgical precision, "two rounds to the body, and one to the head." Threat neutralized. Clearing an L-shaped room exemplifies the need for total confidence in your tactics and in your teammates. The tactics required me to move straight ahead after J.D. lobbed the flash-bang around the corner of the *L*. This was a predetermined move. The concussion, flash, and smoke from the flash-bang would disorient anybody located around the corner. If anyone did try to sight on me with a weapon as I moved across the room, the second operator, who looped the corner, would shoot him.

    I could hear Charlie team moving in our direction through an interior door located next to dead tango number two. I was to link up with the members of Charlie team who had blasted their way into the rear of the crisis site through an exterior cinder block wall. I stood away from the door and yelled, "Charlie, Hotel…link up!" The door cracked and a green Nomex glove poked through with a thumbs-up, followed by, "Charlie, link up." I tightly grasped the Charlie operator's thumb: link-up complete. I heard Dave advise J.D., over the handi-talkie radio, that his room was clear. Dave linked up with Echo team in the same manner. The L-shaped family room was clear, as well as the living room where we had found the hostage. J.D. announced over the radio, "Hotel team, hold what ya got." J.D. physically moved to each room and asked for a count to determine the number of tangos and hostages, live or dead. Dave advised, "One dead tango." The living room called out "One dead tango, one live hostage." I advised "One dead tango." As we held our positions, each operator visually looked around the room for weapons and the presence of undetected Improvised Explosive Devices (IEDs).[9] One unseen trip wire attached to a grenade could ruin your day. J.D. confirmed our counts and then spoke into the radio, "Hotel TL to Alpha One."

"Hotel TL, this is Alpha One, go ahead."

"Alpha One, Hotel is clear," J.D. advised. "We have one live hostage and three dead tangos. Copy?"

"I copy," came the response. "Hotel clear, with one live hostage and three dead tangos. Hotel TL stand by."

Alpha One received similar counts from Charlie, Echo, and Golf teams. When all reports were in, the total was two live hostages and six dead terrorists. Echo team had located the second hostage, a female. She had been extracted from the structure in the same manner as the male hostage we had rescued, and loaded onto the same Little Bird. By now, both hostages were miles from the crisis site.

"Everybody, make 'em safe," was the next command broadcast over the radio by Alpha One. Hearing this, all of the operators depressed the magazine release on their respective MP5s and removed their thirty-round magazines. Each operator also physically racked the action and ejected the live round that was already chambered in his weapon. The MP5s were then left to hang from the harness strap that was slung around each operator's neck. Alpha One directed our attention to where he was standing on the third deck of an observation tower overlooking the "crisis site." Alpha One then stepped up to a microphone positioned adjacent to where he was standing. "Gentlemen, as always, congratulations. Your demonstration of a dynamic hostage rescue was flawless."

Standing next to Alpha One on the tower was FBI Director William Sessions, Acting Attorney General (AG) William Barr, and U.S. Senator Orrin Hatch. In addition, there were a number of straphangers who were busy posturing themselves around each of the VIPs. Acting AG Barr had previously headed the DOJ's Office of Legal Counsel. He was still a key adviser to former AG Richard Thornburg. With Thornburg's departure to mount his Senate campaign, William Barr had been selected to fill his seat until President George Bush named a replacement.

Next would come the standard photo op with an operator and a walk-through review of the breach points and the targets. As the spectators walked through the 10,000-square-foot shooting house, which routinely portrayed a crisis site, some would marvel at the overlapping holes in the targets that represented tangos. A double tap in the heart or right between the eyes always got their attention. There was the occasional timid soul who would grimace and ask, "Why don't they shoot to wound?" The FBI's deadly force policy[10] does not include a shoot to wound option. A wounded subject, just like a wounded animal, is still dangerous and has the capability to kill. In hostage rescue, the threat must be neutralized. The well-being of the hostages depends upon this premise.

And so, the only civilian, full-time, counterterrorist team in the United States ended another demonstration, better known as a demo or dog and pony show. Demos of this type require significant planning and rehearsals. This was the mechanism that would hopefully lead to more deployments, and this demo in particular was meant to convince Congress of the need to enhance the Team's annual budget.

As the VIPs strolled through the shooting house looking at our weapons and our tactical gear, they seemed oblivious to what would follow the assault. No mention was made of who would secure the crime scene, collect the evidence, or interview any survivors. Six dead terrorists meant six Shooting Review Boards, unending public scrutiny, second-guessing by the media, and armchair quarterbacking by every talking head expert CNN could dig up. What the VIPs just witnessed was a demo, but the helicopter insertion, the rounds fired, the explosive breaches, the flash-bangs, and the operators posing as hostages (as rounds passed within inches of their heads) were all live.

The operators had once again entered into the close confines of the live-fire shooting house, carried out their mission of locating and extracting two live hostages, neutralized six terrorists, cleared the entire 10,000-square-foot structure, and emerged unscathed. All of this was accomplished in less than one minute yet required precision teamwork coupled with surgical shooting skills. Indeed, there are a very limited number of counterterrorist teams anywhere in the world with this capability. So went another day of "hard realistic training" for the nation's number one, elite counterterrorist team. The FBI's Hostage Rescue Team, better known as the HRT, was the final option in the event of any high-risk law enforcement action within the continental United States (CONUS).

File No.: Chapter Three
Subject: Honing the Edge

The FBI Academy and the HRT compound are both located within the confines of the U.S. Marine Corps Base at Quantico, Virginia. When I arrived there for the March 1990 HRT selection it was with the awareness that I was about to venture into an elite community. HRT was the big leagues. Similar to the way college athletes are drafted into professional sports, the HRT selection would cull the best-suited candidates from the FBI special agents invited to try out. The FBI consists of approximately 12,000 special agents. A very small percentage of this population apply to become members of the HRT. This can be contributed to one or more of the following reasons: disinterest, inability to meet the physical fitness standards, not wanting to relocate to the Washington DC area, the extensive travel associated with assignment to the HRT, or fear of failure.

On average, the FBI receives one hundred applications per year from candidates requesting an invitation to the HRT selection. Approximately thirty-five FBI SAs are invited to attend the annual selection. Generally, seven to ten candidates, better known as selectees, survive the two-week HRT selection course and are chosen to continue the process. Each selectee must then successfully complete the sixteen-week New Operator Training School, better known as NOTS. Once a selectee enters NOTS, he becomes known as a Not Head and undergoes extensive training in the fundamentals associated with operator tradecraft. Firearms, CQB, mechanical and explosive breaching, physical fitness, land navigation, patrolling, defensive tactics, dignitary protection, emergency/tactical vehicle operation, maritime assault tactics, basic trauma life support, helicopter operations, fast roping, rappelling, and climbing are just a few of the disciplines covered. Rarely does a Not Head wash out. At the end of the sixteen weeks, each Not Head is assigned as an assaulter or as a sniper/observer. When it's all said and done, only one in ten applicants finish NOTS and are assigned permanently to the HRT. Success or failure is based on luck, preparedness, and desire. I knew why I became a member of the HRT. This was my niche in life. God put me on earth to be an operator. The HRT was where I belonged. Three years into my six-year tenure with the HRT, I took charge of the selection process. In fact, while assigned to the HRT, I completed my master's degree in criminal justice, for which my thesis was based on a study of the physical fitness requirements associated with the HRT selection.[11] No one makes it through selection and NOTS without possessing the aptitude and attitude to perform the HRT mission.

Special agents selected to become members of the HRT are, almost without exception, superb street agents. This should come as no surprise. The HRT mission requires individuals with a can-do attitude. The FBI initiated the formation of the HRT in January 1983. In turn, the United States Attorney General authorized the formation of the HRT and the mission was defined to provide a tactical option for extraordinary hostage situations and terrorist activities threatening to occur on a more frequent basis specifically within the confines of the United States. A civilian law enforcement counterterrorism resource was needed due to the federal regulation referred to as the Posse Comitatus Act, which prohibits United States military forces from operating in a law enforcement capacity unless expressly authorized by the Constitution, the president, or an act of

Congress. Between 1983 and the present, the responsibilities of the HRT have expanded, and as a result, the requirements of the Team have evolved simultaneously. The HRT is a multi-faceted resource prepared to provide numerous types of assistance to law enforcement actions wherever they may be needed.

The HRT consists of special agent operators, the front office (also called head shed), and the remaining staff. The front office includes the chain of command. The staff consists of former HRT operators, special agents who have not gone through the HRT selection process, and non-agent support personnel. The term operator is reserved for members of a counterterrorist team (CT) who have completed the rigorous indoctrination: selection and NOTS. The Navy SEALs call it BUD/S. Each CT team worldwide has a term for the indoctrination process used to choose new team members. The operators are the assaulters and sniper/observers; they are the shooters, the gunslingers, the individuals who go through the door or take the shot, the ones laying it on the line.

In today's world of political correctness, the term sniper/observer is often transposed to observer/sniper to soften it for those who are uncomfortable and ignorant of the S/O's mission. S/Os operate as a two-man team, one sniper and one observer. When deployed, the men alternate time spent on the weapon to watch the objective through the rifle's optics. Hours spent looking through a scope take their toll both physically and mentally on the sniper. To provide constant, reliable, and accurate intelligence to the command post, the men pull shifts. Snipers save lives. They provide coverage as the assaulters move to and stage at phase line green. They neutralize imminent threats and defuse volatile situations.

When I recall my selection, one operator, who was both a sniper and an assaulter during his tenure with the HRT, stands out. From the very first morning, as we all gathered for the initial Physical Training (PT) test, SA Dave Corderman was there with us. Throughout the two-week selection he ran, force-marched, swam, climbed, and negotiated every obstacle we encountered. He was one of the "yellow shirts" who volunteered to perform the events with the selectees while he evaluated performance. All of the HRT operators are tasked with evaluating the performance of the selectees through firsthand observation, but some actually participate in the event. While doing this they wear the yellow HRT T-shirt with the letters *HRT* emblazoned over the left side of the chest. Only a few of the operators perform all of the events with the selectees. Dave was one of them.

As Dave and the other operators evaluated our performance, we in turn watched them. Dave never flinched. He not only completed each grueling evolution, but did so while closely watching and listening for weakness, a verbal complaint, or someone whining. During one of the events known as the Quigley, we were challenged with running an obstacle course through a quagmire in the woods and swamps located on the Quantico Marine Corps base. I came up on one obstacle that required me to mount and conduct a combat crawl across a rope, which was strung about ten feet above a tank trap full of stagnant water. The water was about four feet deep. As I started across the rope, I could see Dave out of the corner of my eye. Suddenly the rope began to jerk violently. One of the other operators was pulling on the rope in an effort to make me lose my grip. He succeeded and I plunged headfirst into the murky water. When I stood up, there was Dave with a shit-eating grin on his face. I climbed out of the tank trap attempting to shake the muck out of my eyes and ears. Dave looked at me and said matter-of-factly, "You better catch your group." I took off with Dave running right next to me, watching to see if I'd break. As I ran I thought, "This is the kind of guy I want going through the door with me. This guy feels no pain." Dave Corderman set the standard for me from the beginning. He and I became teammates and, eventually, close friends.

I was a member of Generation Seven or GEN7. Once you become a member of the HRT, your routine training regimen consists of daily and weekly evolutions. Shooting and CQB skills are fundamental to operational readiness and perishable if not routinely practiced. HRT operators shoot, on average, 1000 rounds per week during training and shoot 40 percent of the total annual rounds expended by the entire 12,000 agents employed by the FBI. This statistic reveals several things. First, it underscores the role that repetition plays in honing the edge. Acquiring the surgical shooting skills you need in the close confines of an aircraft fuselage or a congested urban setting takes practice. Second, it explains why HRT operators are highly respected throughout the counterterroism community for their exceptional shooting skills. Third, it indicates that the non-HRT agent doesn't shoot very often. In fact FBI SAs are required to complete firearms training just once every three months, or four times per year.

Well-honed shooting skills notwithstanding, CQB is the real bread and butter of the HRT. All operators cross train to perform this skill. Conducting CQB is what an assaulter does; for sniper/observers, CQB is second only to the skills associated with their sniper rifle. I am an assaulter. I have always been an assaulter. I never wanted to be anything but an assaulter. I equate being an assaulter to being a running back in football. In hostage rescue, the stakes are much higher than on the gridiron, but in both instances, the success of the mission is based on team effort. An integral part of this success is reaching the end zone on the gridiron, or the hotspot (the location of the hostages) in a rescue mission.

When I was a new running back at Ventura Junior College in California, the coach pulled two other running backs and me aside just before the first game of the season. He told us that we would each start a quarter of the game and the one who performed the best would play the fourth quarter. Since I was the newest running back, he assigned me to the third quarter. This pissed me off. I rode the bench for the first half. When halftime rolled around I was determined to get into the game and earn a starting position. We received the second half kickoff and the ball was downed at our own thirty-yard line. When we huddled up, the quarterback called for a 34 dive. This meant I would take a handoff from the quarterback and carry the ball through the line between the strong-side guard and tackle. The intent was to gain one or two yards and establish a ground game. I looked across the huddle at my buddy who played strong-side guard and said, "I'll see you in the end zone." He looked back at me in disbelief.

We approached the line of scrimmage. We were running the "Power I" offense. The quarterback reached under the center and called the snap count. The center snapped the ball to the quarterback who pivoted to his right and handed the ball off to me. I hit the 4 hole. Unfortunately, it was plugged by our strong-side tackle, who, at six foot seven and 350 pounds, happened to be the largest lineman in college football that year. We called him Squeak. I ran into the back of Squeak, spun right, and raced seventy yards off tackle to score. I stood in the end zone and waited for my buddy to get there. I started the fourth quarter and ultimately ran for nearly 200 yards in that game. Whether it's football or hostage rescue, you can damn well guarantee I'll reach the objective.

Years into my assignment to the HRT, I became a CQB instructor. In this role, I adopted three fundamental rules for accomplishing the mission: "get there, get in, and get some." If you break any one of these rules, your chance for success significantly lessens.

The HRT can "get there" by air, land, or sea, or a combination of each. Rotor wing aircraft can deliver the Team by air. If helicopters are utilized, then operators can fast rope, rappel, skid jump, helocast, or exit the helicopter after it touches down. If the Team comes in on the ground, then assault vehicles can be utilized. Assault vehicles include "rigged" Suburbans, extended-cab four-by-four pick-ups, vans, Humvees, Bradley Fighting Vehicles, or armored personnel carriers (APCs). More exotic ground transportation includes motorcycle dirt bikes, all-terrain vehicles (ATVs), or snowmobiles. The Team may elect to move on foot or on snow skis toward the objective. This requires expertise in climbing, mountaineering, land navigation, and patrolling. The Team may come in by water. Maritime options include combat swimming on the surface, employing scuba gear, utilizing a rebreather (bubbleless system), fast boats, inflatable boats, or kayaks. If none of these options can get the Team to the prescribed mission, other unique delivery systems can be explored. This may include, but is not limited to, parachuting from aircraft or "locking out" from a submarine. Whichever delivery mechanism (or combination of delivery mechanisms) is selected, the HRT has the equipment and operators who are experts in providing the needed capability.

For the HRT to "get in" almost always requires the entry team to stage at phase line green and await a countdown. Getting to phase line green is no easy task. Once, in an urban high-rise, I faced surreptitious entry and movement in a dark elevator shaft from the twentieth floor to the crisis location on the thirtieth floor. Another mission had me climbing, undetected, the exterior hull of a luxury cruise liner under the cover of darkness in twenty-foot seas to reach the ship's deck where hostages were being held. In another situation, I had to scale a twenty-foot assault ladder while exercising extreme noise and light discipline, and stage on the top ladder-rung outside the fuselage door of a 747 commercial airliner.

Just like during a demo, the on-scene commander (OSC) initiates the countdown when he determines all assets have reached the breach point and are at green. When this determination is made, the OSC broadcasts the command "All elements are at green. I have control," over the radio. He then begins the countdown starting at five. At two, the snipers engage targets of opportunity, but only if the targets pose an imminent threat to the assaulters, hostages, or other innocent civilians. The OSC then resumes the countdown. At one, the breachers fire their charges, which detonate the explosive breach. Next, the OSC announces, "execute, execute, execute." Hearing this, the assault teams make entry into the crisis site.

Although getting in does not always require external force, in most incidents the breach is accomplished by mechanical or explosive means, or a combination of both. Should you underestimate the surface to be breached and fall short of gaining entry into the crisis site, hostages will die. No matter how the breach is accomplished, the action must be conducted as precisely and as rapidly as possible. Mechanical breaches include the use of battering rams, sledgehammers, bolt cutters, chainsaws, circular saws, shotguns, cutting torches, and assault vehicles equipped with frame-mounted winches. Explosive breaches include premeasured linear shaped charges, water charges, and "slap-shots" designed to create an entry point by pushing, cutting, or blasting a hole in the crisis site. Explosive material is carefully measured to ensure that enough is included to get the job done. To under- or over-estimate the amount of explosive material needed can lead to tragic results. Above all, a fail-safe breach is a mandatory prerequisite to any successful assault. In hostage rescue, the breach of choice is the explosive breach. Not only is entry gained quickly, but the accompanying concussion is an attention getter. This diversion is a prerequisite in order to "get some." When the HRT "gets some," it is analogous to getting the job done. It cannot be understated that the fail-safe breach is critical to assault team success. If the breach fails then the mission is in serious jeopardy. Once entry is made, another concept comes into play. The concepts of "speed, surprise, and violence of action" all contribute to successfully accomplishing the mission (getting some). The mission may be rescuing hostages, arresting terrorists, securing a location to be searched, or a combination of two or more of these objectives.

Speed is required to rapidly secure the crisis site before hostages are killed or before the terrorists have time to react to the assault. You don't sacrifice safety or established protocols to acquire speed. The speed inherent to a successful assault comes only through countless hours of practice and rehearsals. This includes mastering the weapons, the equipment, and the movement associated with CQB. Through repetition, the mind develops muscle memory. You learn through repetition exactly where your handgun is located within the assault holster hanging from your tactical belt and affixed to the outside of your thigh. As a result you can reach for the pistol grip, draw, fire, and holster the weapon without taking your eyes off the threat. The movement becomes instinctive. The speed associated with CQB cannot be accomplished by rushing. The adage "Smooth is Fast" reiterates the essence of how an operator conducts business when disaster or triumph hinges on every second.

Along with speed comes surprise. Surreptitious entry, undetected movement, and noise and light discipline all contribute to gaining the element of surprise. This delayed detection coupled with an explosive breach, diversions, and numerous concussion grenades or flash-bangs all contribute to the shock needed to overwhelm and postpone any reaction by those being assaulted.

Violence of action is accomplished as a byproduct of speed and surprise. In addition, it includes superiority of firepower and personnel, in other words, more guns and operators. Violence is inherent to CQB. When the decision is made to assault a crisis site, negotiations have failed. Initiating an assault includes unleashing a violent response pursuant to the actions of the terrorists. In this instance, the violence is controlled and channeled to accomplish an objective. That objective is to save lives. As the assault team enters and physically moves through the crisis site, the actions of the operators are deliberate, decisive, and, if necessary, deadly. The assault team moves like a steamroller, crushing everything in its path to locate the hostages. The rules of engagement are explicit. Anyone who threatens the lives of the hostages is to be neutralized. This is accomplished by double tapping any threat. Two well-placed rounds to the body (torso) and one round in the head, ensures that the threat is properly addressed. Headshots are not taken initially unless the situation necessitates such. The head is a hard target that is continuously moving. Like a "pumpkin on a post," it's balanced on the shoulders. When the life of a hostage is in imminent danger, a terrorist is shot in the head. This is done in order to instantly kill the terrorist. Taking headshots underscores the absolute requirement that there be no thrown rounds. The margin of error in CQB is zero. All fired rounds must be accounted for. Unlike their military counterparts, the HRT does not factor in acceptable losses, nor does the HRT engage in suppressive fire. In civilian law enforcement, every round fired will be scrutinized in court to determine the justification of a law enforcement officer's actions. HRT operators are FBI special agents and therefore held, at least, to the same standard as all law enforcement officers. To "get there, get in, and get some" requires a proficiency in operator tradecrafts only achieved through continuous and rigorous training. The training cycles not only keep operator skills sharp but also replicate potential mission environments. One of the basic human responses that operators must learn to control is the "flinch." The flinch—the moment of hesitation that results when a person is startled—is what CT operators rely on when they toss a flash-bang into a room or create an explosive diversion. The subsequent moments after the explosion, when the terrorists are incapacitated or surprised, provide the time for the assault force to gain the upper edge. Operators must learn to react instinctively. The flinch will always exist, but you can reduce the moment of hesitation to the point that it is indiscernible. This is accomplished by rehearsing in your mind how you will react to various crisis situations. This means mentally going through the motions of how you will react if confronted. Pro athletes mentally envision catching a pass for a touchdown or hitting a home run. CT operators mentally envision engaging an armed terrorist and successfully placing two rounds in the chest and one in the head.

Most of the HRT training is conducted in-house. The HRT compound is equipped with two state-of-the-art live fire shooting houses, firearms ranges, and access to all of the other training facilities available at the FBI Academy. In addition, being located on the U.S. Marine Corps Base, Quantico provides access to a plethora of training facilities utilized by the Marines. To further enhance its training environment and to maintain liaison between counterterrorism team counterparts around the world, the HRT routinely invites operators from other CT teams to Quantico. In return, these CT teams reciprocate and invite HRT operators to integrate into their training cycles. These opportunities expose the HRT operator to unique training environments and allow for an exchange of ideas and techniques between CT teams. Such an exchange in personnel also instills confidence between CT teams. Counterterrorism team operators are all warriors cut from the same cloth whose dedication to duty and esprit de corps is universal.

After graduating from NOTS in December 1990, I was approached by the HRT assault team supervisor who asked if I would be interested in attending the U.S. Navy's Basic Underwater Demolition/SEAL (BUD/S) Training. I jumped at the chance.

Sunrise on Coronado Island, located off the coast of San Diego, California, is never more glorious than when you experience it while doing "mountain climbers" along with seventy-five U.S. Navy SEAL recruits on the blacktop macadam in preparation for another day of BUD/S. On May 1, 1991, I arrived at the U.S. Naval Special Warfare Center in Coronado, California, with five other HRT operators.

As part of a long-standing exchange between the HRT and the SEALs, I was among six HRT operators selected to attend BUD/S Class 176 during its Dive Phase. The HRT, on an as-needed basis, selects and sends a finite number of operators to integrate into a BUD/S class. The intent is to emerge from the training as a certified Navy Diver, and continue to reinforce the HRT's relationship with the SEALs.

The HRT/SEAL relationship extends back to the genesis of the HRT. When the concept of developing an HRT was proposed, efforts were taken to structure the Team after existing CT teams. These were primarily the Navy SEALs, Army Delta, and the British SAS. Their influence is most notable in the HRT's terminology, organization, and equipment. Every HRT operator understands the importance of keeping his own "kit" in order. This is the term the Brits use to describe an operator's individual gear and equipment. The HRT is divided into two sections: Blue and Gold. The SEALs use the same color designations. The two HRT sections are further divided into assault and sniper teams and each of these teams is given an alpha designator. For example, within the Blue section are two assault teams, Hotel and Echo. Army Special Forces use alpha designators to identify their individual squadrons. The HRT initially adopted the same handgun carried at one time by the British SAS: the 9mm, Browning Hi-Power.

Symbolic of the bond that exists between the HRT and the Navy SEALs is a tribute in the lobby of the Coronado BUD/S compound. The tribute is to Tommy Norris, a recipient of the United States' highest commendation for bravery, the Congressional Medal of Honor. The personification of a CT operator, Tommy is both a former U.S. Navy SEAL and HRT operator.

When approached about attending BUD/S, I knew I would need to partner-up with another operator. In the world of counterterrorism, you always work with a partner. I suggested Big Jack be considered. In addition to surviving HRT selection and NOTS together, Big Jack and I also shared the experience of having played college ball. Jack had played nose guard for West Point, and we both had the road map of scars on our knees representing multiple surgeries to repair torn ACLs, medial collateral ligaments, and the removal of cartilage. During HRT selection, Big Jack and I had provided ringside entertainment for the operators during the boxing evolution. Touted as the heavyweight bout and main event, we succeeded in exchanging blow after blow in a rock 'em, sock 'em display that left us both on the verge of a TKO. Big Jack got the slot, and we teamed up as dive buddies for BUD/S. Throughout selection and NOTS, Big Jack always had a way of maintaining his composure when we all knew another grueling evolution was on the horizon. Big Jack would announce, "Stand by to SUCK…SUCK," and that was what we would each end up doing. Sucking it up through another evolution. This attitude would serve the six of us well during BUD/S.

The SEALs define the warrior creed, and nowhere is this better exemplified than during the six-month BUD/S indoctrination. BUD/S is SEAL boot camp. The process is divided into four phases. The first phase a SEAL recruit is exposed to is Phase Four, the Preconditioning Phase. During this phase, the SEAL recruit undergoes a series of tests, both physical and psychological. The purpose of Phase Four is to get the recruits to a level of fitness that will allow them to survive the following three phases.

Next is Phase One, the Physical Conditioning Phase, which includes the infamous Hell Week. Because this is one of the experiences that all SEALs share, it fosters a brotherhood among the SEAL community that lasts a lifetime. Hell Week is best described as a continuous 150-hour evolution of extreme physical and mental torment augmented with sleep and food deprivation. The objective is to push the recruits beyond any physical or mental limitations they thought they had.

Next comes Phase Two, the Dive Phase. This phase introduces the recruit to the physics of diving in a classroom environment and teaches him how to operate underwater with both open and closed circuit dive systems. This phase, more than any other, tests the recruit's resolve not to panic when exposed to extreme stress. The Dive Phase culminates with an evolution known as Pool Comp. Second only to Hell Week in terms of attrition, Pool Comp provides an environment where the recruit is wet, cold, and fatigued. In addition, the recruit is disoriented and visibility is, at best, minimal. All of these discomforts exponentially increase when you realize that Pool Comp occurs in twenty feet of water where the ability to breath is optional.

The final phase, Phase Three, is the Land Warfare Phase. Conducted on San Clemente Island, this phase focuses on conventional and special weapons training. The phase culminates with a field training exercise (FTX) that incorporates all aspects of the SEAL recruits' training to date.

The BUD/S recruits were just beginning Phase Two when we arrived. Several of my HRT peers in attendance were already certified divers. I, on the other hand, had never had a scuba diving lesson in my life. In some ways, I considered this a blessing; just like going through the unknowns of HRT selection, sometimes ignorance is bliss. Plus, I hadn't had a chance to develop any bad habits. I was relying on the U.S. Navy to certify me as a diver, and learning this skill gratis made the Navy SEALs seem like a great opportunity. On the first day of dive physics, I noticed immediately that the average age of BUD/S Class 176 was about twenty-three. This was to be expected since most of the students were enlisted sailors right out of the fleets. We six, on the other hand, had an average age of thirty-five. Ten plus years older than the average SEAL recruit. Still, the SEAL recruits, as well as the SEAL instructors, would soon learn this age difference would have zero impact on our physical performance. A prerequisite for an HRT operator to attend BUD/S is completing two hours of continuous physical exercise, which includes 600 flutter kicks, a two-mile combat swim (with fins) in under seventy minutes, and a four-mile run in under twenty-eight minutes. This is in addition to our normal standards, which includes push-ups, pull-ups, sit-ups, a thirty-foot rope climb, and a 120-yard shuttle run.

An understanding of dive physics is a prerequisite before getting wet. As Phase Two got underway, we attended a barrage of classroom instruction, which focused on understanding the dos and don'ts of diving. This included diving physics, anatomy and physiology, diving diseases (hypoxia, oxygen toxicity, carbon monoxide poisoning, nitrogen narcosis, hypothermia, decompression sickness, and arterial gas embolism), attack boards hand signals, diving logs and air diving tables, plus a lot more. Classroom instruction at BUD/S is unique. A wrong answer or the occasional dozing off, which comes with long hours and little sleep, results in a quick trip to the "dip tank," or a trip out to the shore break where the recruit gets the chance to become a sugar cookie. In other words, dive into the Pacific, get out of the water, and roll in the sand. This is done while wearing the uniform of the day. Usually, this keeps the sleepy student alert. In one instance, a young sailor just couldn't stay awake. He was directed to stand up throughout the class. This didn't seem like that big of a deal; of course he was wet and sandy, but he was directed to stand in a tub of ice. He still fell asleep.

Classroom instruction at BUD/S is geared toward high school graduates. As HRT operators, and FBI special agents, we all had college degrees, so the academics were a review of Physics 101 in many cases. Each day we promptly reported to class wearing our white HRT polo shirts with the FBI seal, and khaki-colored cargo pants. We sat in the last row of seats, elevated above the rest of the class. During breaks, we would go outside into the breezeway and pass the time doing sets of dips, pull-ups, push-ups, and sit-ups. The other students saw what we were doing and started joining in. The BUD/S instructors interpreted this to mean they weren't working the class hard enough during PT since the students had enough energy to exercise during breaks. I'm sure the students paid for it later when we weren't around.

During BUD/S, there is little differentiation between the enlisted and commissioned students. If anything, the officers are expected to assume a leadership role during the BUD/S process. Leadership is a vital characteristic that the officers who will lead men into harm's way must possess. Leadership within the FBI, on the contrary, is an anomaly, especially outside the paramilitary environment of the HRT. Joining the ranks of FBI management requires nothing more than filling out an application and then brownnosing the entity who decides who gets the job. One nitwit "manager" told me that "the phone calls made behind the scenes" are what really matter when applying for promotions within the FBI. The frightening thing is this same nitwit and many others like him have already, or are still, rising within the ranks of the bureau. It is by happenstance when a person who is promoted within the FBI possesses leadership traits. During my career, I worked for countless managers. I can count the leaders on one hand.

Concurrent with classroom instruction is a battery of physical fitness (PT) evolutions. These consist of timed four to seven-mile beach runs, deep sand runs, obstacle courses, calisthenics, and two-mile ocean swims. The other HRT operators and I were well conditioned for the PT. One of us usually finished first on the timed runs and we always finished near the front during the swims. Big Jack had a lot of heart, but he wasn't the fastest swimmer and we always swam with our swim buddy. Big Jack usually wore glasses and when we hit the water his vision significantly diminished. The swims usually required us to go out approximately a quarter mile and then turn and parallel the shoreline during the swim. A boat would be positioned at the one-mile mark (nautical mile, which is farther). This was our turnaround point. During the timed two-mile surface swims, I would always face the shore to keep Big Jack and me on track. Between strokes, Big Jack would ask me, "How much farther to the turnaround?" I would respond, "About fifty yards, Big Jack." Ten minutes later Big Jack would say, "Scarhead, how much farther to the turnaround?" I would respond, "Oh, about fifty yards, Big Jack." Big Jack knew the answer was always fifty yards, but he still liked to ask.

During one of the swims I teamed up with another HRT operator who had been a collegiate swimmer. I never swam competitively, but growing up in Florida allowed me to spend a lot of time in the water. I also surfed for many years, which really conditions the shoulders for swimming. We finished second on that swim, and if we hadn't had a mishap, we probably would have finished first. About three-quarters of the way through, my false teeth came loose and shot out of my mouth when I exhaled. Miraculously I caught them before they hit the water. I handed them to my swim buddy who was wearing neoprene gloves. He shoved them into one of his gloves and we kept going.

Later back in the classroom, the six of us were asked to remain outside while the instructors spoke to the rest of the class. The BUD/S instructor could be heard through the closed door of the classroom screaming at the top of his lungs. I overheard him say to the class, "Do you realize those HRT guys are old enough to be your fathers? What do you think the president is going to say when he hears they're kicking your ass in PT?" I figured this was just another motivational speech to the recruits, and our presence gave the instructors some new ammunition to work with.

When the classroom portion of the phase ended, we began a series of dives, which would eventually culminate with Pool Comp. One of the more memorable dives for me was the gear exchange, which was conducted in the dive pool. Big Jack and I were issued one set of twin 80 dive tanks, and one regulator equipped with a mouthpiece and inhalation and exhalation hoses. We each had our own mask, fins, KA-BAR knife with sheath, and weight belt. We were told in the classroom that our equipment was similar to the system Jacques Cousteau invented, the same man responsible for freeing mankind from the confines of land and opening up the world beneath the sea for exploration. They meant it; in fact, it looked like Jacques had used some of this exact gear. Having never dived before, it didn't really make a difference to me, but the other guys were freaking out. Once again, ignorance is bliss, or so I thought.

When Big Jack and I hit the water for the gear exchange evolution, we were both feeling pretty confident. We made our way to the bottom of the pool while buddy breathing off of one rig. This was no big deal. We had practiced this technique at Quantico and also here before this evolution. The technique requires two divers, one with a rig on, to swim side by side and take turns breathing off the same mouthpiece. As long as the equipment functioned, no problem, but then Murphy stepped in and things started going wrong. Big Jack and I positioned ourselves on the bottom of the pool in order to exchange the gear from him to me and then back again. I noticed the hose was full of water each time Big Jack handed me the mouthpiece. The best I could do was get a couple of inhalations and hand the mouthpiece back to Big Jack. Not surprising since these rigs had been through countless Pool Comps where the hoses were stretched out of proportion. As a result, many of the hoses had holes in them. This was no big deal with the left side exhalation hose. If it goes down you can exhale through your nose. The inhalation hose is another story. You more or less need it to breathe. This dilemma continued, and each time Big Jack handed me the mouthpiece, I would swallow all of the pool water in the hose and then try to get a breath. Of course, Big Jack would be grasping for the mouthpiece by this time and seeing his eyes starting to bug out of his head convinced me to hand him the mouthpiece. Each time, I got less air and the law of diminishing returns started to take effect. In other words, I was slowly drowning. The BUD/S instructors are always in the vicinity and I could see them circling my position as I slowly began to exhibit the symptoms of oxygen deprivation. First the tunnel vision began and then my body began twitching. The next thing I knew, I had an instructor wrapping his arms around me from the rear and squeezing my diaphragm as we surfaced. This was to keep me from embolizing. When we reached the side of the pool, they hoisted me out. I came around and sat up on the side of the pool. The instructor next to me said, "Are you okay?"

"Yeah…" I sputtered, "…as far as I can tell."

"Good," he said. "Get back in the pool and finish the evolution."

So there I was back on the bottom of the pool, less than five minutes after experiencing "shallow water blackout." Big Jack was grasping for the mouthpiece again. This time I pulled back and thought to myself, "Sorry dive buddy, but I ain't going through that again." We both learned to hold our breath a little longer that day and successfully passed that evolution.

When our six weeks at BUD/S concluded, I left Coronado with a great respect for the SEAL community and the BUD/S experience. This would not be the last time I would train and work with the SEALs, and I would always have a portion of the shared BUD/S experience to reflect upon.

It was mid-June 1991 when the six of us arrived back at the HRT Compound. We each integrated back into our respective assault and sniper teams to continue honing our individual skills. Little did we know tensions were simultaneously building inside

Federal Correctional Institution (FCI) Talladega, Alabama, among a group of violent Cuban inmates. These were some of the same inmates who had rioted at United States Penitentiary (USP) Atlanta and FCI Oakdale in November 1987. The HRT had responded to both of these incidents, but the resolution was accomplished through verbal negotiations. Unfortunately, FCI Talladega would soon erupt and the HRT would be tested like never before.

File No.: Chapter Four
Subject: When the Balloon Goes Up

During the American Civil War and both World War I and II, observation balloons were hoisted to assist with spotting artillery barrages and detecting troop movement on the battlefield. Balloons were also raised, in lieu of using couriers, to notify gunners to open fire. Eventually the phrase "When the balloon goes up" became synonymous with the implication of pending trouble. On Wednesday, August 21, 1991, "the balloon went up" for the HRT.

It was a routine Wednesday that began with the eight o'clock morning meeting inside the HRT classroom. Nothing of significance transpired and, like most days, the training schedule included a split cycle. I was assigned to Hotel team, which along with Echo team was part of Blue section. We would spend the morning session in the shooting house conducting CQB, and the afternoon session out on the firearms range. Around 11:00 a.m., we finished with CQB and picked up the shot targets in the shooting house for the afternoon session.

After CQB, it was off to the gym for some PT. This almost always included a run (of various distances), an hour of lifting weights (different body parts on different days), and abdominal exercises. Each day as I headed to the gym, my assaulter brother, Nick, would ask, "Hey, Scarhead, what's the workout today?" I would respond, "Today it's run, lift, then abs." Every day Nick would ask the same question and every day I would vary my response. "Today it's lift, run, and abs." Just because the routine was always the same didn't mean I couldn't do it in a different order.

We never made it to the afternoon firearms session. Simultaneous to our cleaning of the shooting house, a group of Cuban inmates vowing "freedom or death" had forcefully overpowered the guards within the Alpha Unit at the Federal Correctional Institution (FCI) Talladega, Alabama. Upon receiving notification of the uprising, the HRT commander gave the order to broadcast an immediate callback page to all Team pagers. A three-digit code was typed in and transmitted to all operators and support elements for the Team.

You always keep your pager with you, even during workouts, and when it goes off it's usually a test page or your wife wanting to know what time you'll be home. Not this time. I was finishing my run to the "Belly of the Beast" and back. This five-mile run is named for the topography of the Northern Virginia area, which offers significant relief to runners. I received the page, which was routine enough, but seldom did I receive the 777, which meant this wasn't a drill.

My first reaction was to pick up the pace and get back to the locker room. I tried to recall any breaking news from the day before, but nothing came to mind. Still, I didn't panic. Instead, I thought about how many times I had responded to an emergency during the course of a workout as a member of the firefighters (or Helishots) assigned to the Rose Valley Flight Crew[12] in the Los Padres National Forest of Southern California. Routinely we would get word midway through a ten-to-thirteen-mile run advising that a fire had erupted. We would race toward base camp and a bus would be deployed to pick us up. Each morning we would stage our gear on the bus prior to our daily PT in the event of an emergency breaking out before we were through exercising. As soon as we jumped on the bus, it was mass pandemonium as we rushed to get our gear on. The SOP for the Helishots was to be on board our Bell 212 helicopter and lifting off within two minutes of the fire alarm. Many times the rotors were turning and the bird was beginning to lift off as we leapt aboard.

I entered the locker room and saw several other operators grabbing their clothes. I pulled mine out of my locker, stuffed them into my gym bag and headed out the door toward the HRT building. I found my TL, J.D., by his desk in the Blue section's assault team room. Whenever events got tense, J.D.'s arms would begin to elevate. At peak moments of stress, J.D.'s arms would reach a "high hover," almost perpendicular to his body. When I found him, they were already at a "medium hover."

J.D. saw me and barked out an order. "Scarhead, get the ladder packages ready and make sure the Suburbans are good to go. There's going to be a warning order given in the classroom in a few minutes."

The scuttlebutt passing between operators was that a prison riot, like the ones at USP Atlanta and FCI Oakdale, was occurring at FCI Talladega. I went into the back room where the team cages were located. This was where each assault and sniper team kept its individual team and operator equipment stowed. The cages were constructed of floor-to-ceiling, chain-link metal. Each operator had various kit bags packed and color-coded with a piece of tubular nylon. The color of the tubular nylon indicated which assault or sniper team the bag belonged to. Stitched on the tubular nylon was the individual operator's alpha number. My number was 74. An alpha number is assigned to each HRT operator. This is the operator's radio call sign and is used when communicating. For operational security reasons, real names are not used. Along with the alpha number was another color code indicating what kind of gear the bag contained. White denoted that the bag was packed for a cold-weather environment, blue meant maritime, green meant woodland/jungle, and so on.

Operators were scurrying about, ensuring that their bags were appropriately packed. Everyone was busy with the task at hand. No joking among the ranks. Prepping for a mission intensifies the seriousness that already exists among CT operators. The sound of actions being racked and reracked on various caliber firearms could be heard echoing down the hallway. Kit bags were being toted into the garage where they would be placed on pallets in preparation for movement to the location of whichever mode of transportation would take the Team to the scene of the crisis.

As far as I could tell, this operation was going to be contained to a jail facility. This didn't negate the chance another crisis could occur somewhere else, thus requiring the Team to divert to another operation in a different climate. During the winter of 1994, I went from the tropical jungle environment of San Juan, Puerto Rico, where we took out a drug gang terrorizing the local community, to the *Ice Station Zebra* conditions of Northern Michigan in search of some white separatists alleged to belong to the Michigan Militia. Talk about a shock to the system. You have to be ready for anything.

I passed through the cage area on my way to the garage. Parked inside the garage were two mount-out trucks: the red one belonged to Gold section and the white one belonged to Blue section. Each truck was configured to carry all the additional equipment that goes with the Team during a deployment. This included each individual team's gun box that contained specialized weapons: M79 grenade launchers for deploying CS gas, a suppressed 9mm MP5 for reducing the chance of compromise, a .22-caliber pistol for neutralizing dogs, several Remington 12-gauge shotguns for breaching, and each individual operator's .223-caliber Car-15 rifle. Each mount-out truck also included additional mechanical and explosive breaching gear, ballistic shields, a quantity of meals ready to eat (MREs), flares, smoke grenades, flash-bangs, fast ropes, rappelling ropes, and a sundry of other equipment, not least of which were two aluminum storage boxes full of ladder accessories.

I was responsible for the HRT ladder system. This was a project I inherited when I was first assigned to Hotel team. As a former firefighter, this project could not have been assigned to anyone better. Whether or not J.D. took this into consideration when he made the assignment, I don't know. In any case, it was my responsibility to ensure that the ladder system was 100 percent squared away. As a former firefighter, I took very seriously the saying, "Take care of your gear and your gear will take care of you." Along with the ladder system, I was also responsible for researching, developing, and maintaining the various assault accessories, which affixed to the HRT Suburbans. Each assault and sniper team was assigned two Chevrolet/GMC Suburbans. These were our primary assault vehicles. In other words, these were the vehicles that we would use, in most cases, to move up to a crisis site. Various accessories attached to these vehicles: a roof platform, a hood platform, and running boards for carrying personnel. Other equipment included push bars, a 20,000-pound capacity winch, a roof-access ladder, a weapon storage box, and a system that attached to the platforms for deploying ladders. When the Suburbans were fully equipped they looked like something out of a *Mad Max* movie.

The ladder system and the assault vehicles are fundamental to "getting there" and "getting in." If either of these systems fails, the mission is in jeopardy. The ladder inventory consists of four packages of ladders. Two packages each were stored on top of the respective mount-out truck. As I climbed up on top of one of the trucks to make sure all the ladders were intact, I saw my Hotel teammate, Dave Corderman, passing by. Along with him was one of my partners from BUD/S training, Mark. I don't think I ever met a guy who was more serious about his job.

Mark was a former Marine and a consummate professional. At the time, Mark was assigned as a sniper, but, just like Dave, he was one of those operators who could do anything he was tasked with. This is one of the great things about the HRT. You are surrounded by literally the best of the best. You never hear about an operator leaving the FBI to join the military, but we had guys from each of the military services who had resigned to become an HRT operator. A couple of years later, Mark would further demonstrate his diversity as an operator when he and I would attend a winter course at the Marine Corps Mountain Warfare Training Center (MCMWTC) in Pickle Meadows, California. As my "mountain buddy" during training, Mark was truly in his element. We spent many a night huddled together in a snow cave hoping an avalanche didn't bury us for good. While we were there, Mark was promoted to Major in the USMC Reserves. Just as the Navy had taught me to scuba dive at BUD/S, the Marines taught me to snow ski at MCMWTC.

As I was asking Dave and Mark to give me a hand with inventorying the ladders, an announcement came over the intercom directing all operators to the classroom. I jumped down from the top of the truck and the three of us headed back into the building. We entered the classroom for an "all hands" meeting. All the gunslingers were poised to hear what our mission was. The assault supervisor came through the door first, followed by HRT Commander Dick Rogers. Everybody who could find one took a seat. "Gentlemen, we have a mission," the HRT commander began.

Dick Rogers was technically an assistant special agent in charge (ASAC) within the management ranks of the FBI. He answered directly to the special agent in charge (SAC) of the Washington

Field Office (WFO). Since the HRT is a national asset, many times the HRT commander communicates directly with the HBOs (high bureau officials) at FBI Headquarters (FBIHQ). Dick Rogers was the kind of boss who believed in chain of command, and I had no problem with that. In fact, this is a necessary prerequisite for leadership. You can't have an open-door policy and invite every swinging dick to come into your office and voice his likes and dislikes. This is especially true when the guy behind the desk can't ever say no. Ultimately two or more people who have been told yes (to requests that conflict with each other) are going to butt heads. A true leader knows how and when to say no. A true leader also has confidence in his subordinates and allows them the chance to handle matters first before becoming involved. These are rare traits within the management ranks of the FBI where micromanagers prevail and continually interfere.

My experience has shown that micromanagement is the management style of choice for individuals who have risen to a level far beyond their capabilities. These individuals know they're in over their heads, so they focus on the most elementary administrative minutiae, which makes life miserable for everyone. It interferes with accomplishment of the mission and it destroys morale. During my career, I often wondered how anything got accomplished within the FBI. The truth is it got done because of the work ethic of the experienced street agent. Every success the FBI achieves can be credited to the dedicated, determined, doggedness of the special agents "in the weeds" who have their suit coats off and their sleeves rolled up.

Dick Rogers continued, "It looks like we have a situation not much different from the ones in '87 at USP Atlanta and FCI Oakdale. I've been on the phone with Director Sessions. He's been consulting with Acting Attorney General Barr and they want us staged at FCI

Talladega ASAP. Apparently, a group of Cuban inmates, maybe some of the same individuals from before, overpowered their guards and took some hostages. I'm not going to go into a lot of detail. The assault supervisor will do that next when he gives you the warning order. Men, this is the type of job this team was designed to handle. As always, we will conduct ourselves as quiet professionals. Let your wives know you may be gone for a while." Dick Rogers always liked to refer to the Team as "quiet professionals." It meant we, as operators, didn't wait around for accolades after a mission was completed. It was in and out and then onto the next job.

With that, Commander Rogers left the room and the assault team supervisor stood up. This was a guy the entire Team had great respect for. Also a former Marine, his demeanor was always direct and decisive. When he faced the troops, he had his game face on.

"All right, here's what we got. I'll know more when I hear from the advance team." An advance team had departed for Talladega right after ASAC Rogers got the call from the director. The advance consisted of three groups: the S-2 (this is the support element that handles intelligence), the S-3 (the element that handles operations and training), and the S-4 (the Four Shop addresses all the logistics involved with a deployment). In addition to the groups, the advance included an assault team rep, a sniper team rep, a breacher, and a guy from the medical shop. Once on the ground, the advance team would report back with the latest intelligence specific to the crisis. This information was crucial in terms of which specialized equipment we would need in the mount-out.

The assault supervisor continued, "For now, we know that at approximately 1000 hours, a group of Cuban inmates, who are housed in a secure wing at FCI Talladega, overpowered their guards and took eleven hostages. FBI Birmingham is on scene. Bureau of

Prisons (BOP) has one of their Special Operations Response Teams (SORTs) on hand, and they're maintaining a perimeter along with local law enforcement." This meant the FBI SWAT team in Birmingham along with regional assets from Atlanta and Knoxville were either on scene or en route.

"Listen, guys, you've seen these Cubans before. Some of the same ones involved in the Atlanta and Oakdale riots were shipped to Talladega. They have the same demand. They don't want to be shipped back to Cuba." The Cuban inmates were part of the flood of refugees who had arrived in the United States as part of the Mariel boatlift in 1980. Castro didn't miss an opportunity to dump mental patients and convicted violent felons on the United States. For the HRT to be called upon to clean up someone else's mess was normal. This time eleven lives were at stake.

The assault supervisor concluded by saying, "All right, this is a full-Team deployment. The advance is working up an emergency assault plan (EAP) as we speak. We'll go on shift as soon as we hit the ground there. The Four Shop will meet us at the airport with vehicles and details about where we're staging. Now, let's get a time hack. I have 1425 hours. Each TL let me know when you're up and ready to move to Andrews. I want to be wheels up by 1800 hours. We go on shift tonight. Any questions?" There were none. Everyone knew the HRT has a standing order to be wheels up within four hours after receiving notification of a mission.

Andrews Air Force Base is located just over the Woodrow Wilson Bridge, east of Washington DC. This was where the HRT mustered prior to an airlift. An Air Force C-141 aircraft was always on standby in the event the HRT needed to deploy by cargo plane. That was exactly how we were going to deploy, and preparing for a full HRT deployment by 1800 hours would be like moving a three-ring circus.

As the meeting ended, all the assault supervisor saw was a bunch of assholes and elbows moving toward the door to get ready.

Each of the four assault teams would be responsible for deploying one of their two Suburbans. The Suburbans left behind would remain at the HRT compound. One of the HRT assault team Suburbans being deployed was equipped to function as an ambulance. This vehicle had the backseats removed to accommodate a backboard, a medical kit, oxygen tanks, bags of saline solution for transfusions, and other emergency medical necessities needed in the event of a medical evacuation (medevac). In addition, the two mount-out trucks would also be deployed. All of the individual operator kit bags were placed on the back of a flatbed truck and covered with a blue tarp. Individual operator MP5s, helmet bags, and personal bags were loaded into the back of each assault team's Suburban. All of the sniper weapons, in their hard cases, were loaded on another flatbed truck, secured, and covered with a tarp.

The ladder packages, which were secured on the top of the mount-out trucks, were off-loaded. Each package was placed in a reinforced canvas bag and one package each was reloaded on top of the assault platform affixed to the top of the Suburbans. This was done to meet the height requirements of the C-141's rear fuselage cargo door. The large reinforced canvas bags, commonly called "ladder condoms," also hid the ladders from the public's eye. A fully equipped Suburban with a ladder package secured to the top would not be confused with a crew of painters going to a job. Masking the ladders was for operational security (OPSEC)[13] and protection from the elements. Finally, all of the cold-weather kit bags were placed on a pallet in the HRT building garage. This would allow for a quick load-out of the cold-weather gear in the event another operation came up while the team was on this deployment.

By this time, it was around 1530 hours. I found Dave Corderman and we jumped into the Hotel team Suburban, which was also assigned to me as my take-home vehicle. Within my neighborhood, just outside the back gate of Quantico, it was commonplace to see the neighborhood street lined with dark blue Suburbans with tinted windows. This was a clue that the vehicle belonged either to an HRT operator or a Secret Service Counter Assault Team (CAT) member. I drove and Dave rode shotgun. Nick was assigned the responsibility of maintaining and driving Blue section's white mount-out truck. Nick and Big Jack, who were both on Echo assault team, jumped in the truck to make the trip north to Andrews Air Force Base. Whenever the mount-out trucks deployed, another vehicle went along as an escort. In the event of a breakdown, the second vehicle would be there to assist, given the inventory of equipment maintained inside the mount-out trucks.

Dave and I departed the HRT compound at around 1545 hours with the white mount-out truck in tow. We would need anywhere from one to two hours to make the trip to Andrews, depending on traffic. In preparation for the afternoon rush hour, the I-95 HOV lanes would be running in the opposite direction coming out of Washington DC. We always had the option of throwing a blue light up on the dash and running code. The mount-out truck had a light bar over the cab for this purpose. As we pulled out onto I-95 northbound, the traffic was reasonably light. Hopefully, since we were going against the daily commute into DC this volume of traffic would remain the same. One accident or stalled vehicle would change the flow of traffic immediately and turn the interstate into a parking lot. Still, running code was a last option. A convoy of dark blue Suburbans heading north with lights and sirens activated would attract every ambulance chaser in Northern Virginia. As Dave and I headed north, we kept the white mount-out truck visible in our rearview mirror. We also had direct comms via the BU radio in both vehicles.

In 1987, Dave had deployed with the HRT to both USP Atlanta and FCI Oakdale. I asked him what he thought about the mission we were about to take on and how it compared to those of 1987. Dave, being a very astute individual who always reflects for a minute before he responds to questions, thought for a second and then said, "Jim, I think the Cubans are in a no-win situation, even though they were able to negotiate a surrender in both cases in 1987 and achieve some of their demands. Now they've gone and done the same thing again—they've shown they have the propensity for violence, and they'll kill to get what they want. I thought we were going in at Atlanta, but at the last second, the negotiators worked out a deal. I'm not sure that can be accomplished again."

In fact, the HRT deployed first to FCI Oakdale in 1987 as a result of a Cuban inmate uprising. Almost simultaneous to this incident, the Cuban inmates housed at the United States Penitentiary (USP) in Atlanta erupted and took hostages. Since the HRT was already committed to the FCI Oakdale uprising, the U.S. Army's 1st Special Forces Operational Detachment-Delta (1stSFOD-D), better known as Delta Force, was called in to handle the USP Atlanta uprising. This was accomplished by relaxing the Posse Comitatus Act, which substantially limits the powers of the federal government to use the military for law enforcement inside the United States. Once the FCI Oakdale incident was quelled through negotiations, the HRT deployed to USP Atlanta and assumed the tactical lead there. Even though an assault seemed eminent at USP Atlanta, ultimately the uprising was also resolved through negotiations.

I always respected Dave's comments. The quintessential operator, I thought to myself as I recalled a story he'd told me about a deployment in the mid-1980s. Dave was assigned as a sniper then. He was manning a sniper/observer position located in a rural, high-elevation, cold-weather environment. During the night, temperatures dropped to well below zero degrees Fahrenheit. As a sniper, Dave was required to remain in a fixed position and not move. If Dave moved, he tempted compromise by the subjects he was surveilling. As Dave lay there in his position, he could feel frostbite setting into his extremities, especially his hands. He would need his hands and fingers to pull the trigger on his bolt-action .308-caliber rifle if the need arose. Dave being Dave, he did what had to be done. Given that normal body temperature is 98.6 degrees Fahrenheit, he slipped his hands down by his groin and occasionally urinated on them to keep them from freezing. When Dave told this story to guys on the Team, a lot of them busted his balls. I didn't. He did what had to be done to stay functional. I also know for a fact that the guys who were busting Dave's balls are the same guys who piss in their wetsuits every time they get into cold water.

The trip north was without incident. I was a little surprised. It would have been just like Murphy to jump in and orchestrate a flat tire, a traffic jam, or some other obstacle that would have put us all behind the power curve. Standard procedure was to muster in the parking lot across the street from the main gate at Andrews. We would line up the vehicles and move as a conga line past the gate and out to the tarmac in preparation for loading onto the plane. By 1700 hours, everyone had arrived in the parking lot, and it looked like we were still in good shape to make the 1800-hour deadline. The vehicles lined up in the order they would be loaded onto the C-141. As we moved through the gate, each of us pulled out our "creds" and flashed the Air Force sentry who was assigned to the front gate at Andrews. These guys knew something was up whenever we mustered across the street and started this process. I'm surprised CNN didn't have a contact in the vicinity who could give them a heads-up that something newsworthy was about to break.

Leading the way was one of the Team load masters. These are operators who are U.S. military-trained and certified to load the vehicles and equipment onto the plane. They work in concert with the flight crew, who are also load masters. The Team load master, Beef, was a guy who came on the HRT with me.

Beef, as the nickname suggests, was a large individual. At six foot six, he had easily carried 270 pounds of body weight as an offensive tackle for the Naval Academy. When we tried out for the HRT together, I actually weighed more than Beef. While he tipped the scales at 205 pounds, I was still at my playing weight of 210 pounds. Beef put some pounds back on and got back up to around 250, but he maintained a grueling workout routine. At least once per week he would run from the FBI Academy to I-95 and back. This was, in total, about ten miles. Then he would jump on his bike and ride forty miles. He'd follow this up with either a swim or a session in the weight room. What amazed me is that he would do it in the hot Virginia summer. When it came to self-discipline and meticulous attention to detail, Beef set the standard. Beef was assigned as a sniper/observer, and you always knew when Beef was occupying a sniper position. He would provide a constant dialogue of details to the Sniper Tactical Operations Center (S-TOC). Every descriptive detail of the crisis site and absolutely any activity would be reported by Beef and placed in the sniper log.

Once during a deployment in 1992, I saw Beef sitting at a table in the Team staging area. Beef was scheduled to go out and occupy a sniper position for forty-eight hours. On the table in front of him was enough food to feed an eight-man assault team. He had a whole roasted chicken, a loaf of bread, various kinds of fruit, a gallon of milk, and assorted other treats. He was in the process of consuming everything on the table. I asked him, "Beef, what's up with the smorgasbord you're wolfing down?" He looked up at me and said matter-of-factly, "I'm going out for a couple of days, and I'd rather carry all my meals in my stomach then lug everything in a pack." Hey, that works for me. Why deal with a "drag bag" when you can just pack it away in your gut? Beef is an amazing individual.

Beef gave us the signal, and the drivers lined up their respective vehicles in preparation for moving out to the flight line. With Beef in the lead, we continued the conga line out onto the tarmac where the C-141 was staged with its rear cargo door open and down. Ramps were attached to accommodate the vehicles we would drive up and into the fuselage. Each HRT vehicle had its gross weight displayed and readily visible above the front driver's side fender well. The weight was necessary to calculate where each vehicle would be positioned inside the plane and to ensure that we didn't exceed the weight limitations for the aircraft.

The vehicles were not merely driven onto the plane. Each vehicle was backed on. One of the flight crew load masters would position himself about fifty yards from the back of the aircraft. Each driver would then, upon the command of the load master, swing around and line his vehicle up behind the plane. The load master would then slowly provide hand signals to the driver, directing him back toward the rear cargo doors of the plane. Once the back tires of the vehicle touched the bottom of the ramp leading up into the fuselage, it was incumbent on the driver to keep the steering wheel straight. Side and rearview mirrors cannot be used. The driver must focus on the directional hand signals from the load master. The driver must also keep the gas steady as he backs up the ramp. One jerk of the steering wheel or a heavy foot on the gas could be disastrous. If a vehicle struck the side of the plane, the plane would be immediately grounded. This would potentially jeopardize the mission. Even more worrisome for the individual driver, was the gallery of operators standing by and watching. Occasionally a driver is required to pull back down the ramp for a second try, which results in a chorus of jeers from the onlookers. Operators tend to view everything as a challenge and absolutely hate to screw up. An operator buddy of mine, known as The Kid, put it best when he said, "Scar, operators do everything in excess. They train, they fight, they compete, and they party in excess." The Kid was right.

Once the vehicles are aboard the plane, they are secured to the floor with chains that wrap around the axles and fasten to D-rings on the floor. Next, the back ramp of the C-141 is raised. Kit bags, sniper rifles, and all other miscellaneous gear are loaded onboard, covered with a cargo net, and then secured with cargo straps. Anyone who isn't onboard by this time gets aboard and takes a seat. Seating is provided along the interior wall of the fuselage in the form of canvas bench seats that fold down and secure to the aircraft floor. The rear cargo door and all other hatches are closed and secured.

As I sat there on the bench seat, I made sure my "soft" earplugs were tightly in place. They were a necessity while working on the flight-line loading the plane. Most of my high-decibel hearing was already gone from countless hours spent on the firing range, not to mention my days as a wildland firefighter with constant exposure to chainsaws and helicopter jet engines. As we taxied in preparation for takeoff, I thought about my wife and precious little girl. They were both at home safe and sound. I had confirmed this on the phone in the pilots' lounge just before we loaded the plane. I felt the sensation as the plane gained speed down the runway and became airborne. What was to come was uncertain, but I had confidence in my training, and I knew this type of deployment was why I had chosen to be an HRT operator. I heard the wheels of the plane rise. I glanced down at my wristwatch: the time was 1758 hours.

File No.: Part Two
Subject: Stand By, Stand By

All warriors long to practice their tradecraft during a real-world crisis. The FCI Talladega hostage crisis provided the FBI HRT with this opportunity and challenged its capabilities like never before.

File No.: Chapter Five
Subject: Hurry Up and Wait

As HRT operators, we all knew the potential mission awaiting us was dangerous. It's the nature of the beast within the counterterrorism business, and, as operators, it's what we train for day after day. Now a crisis was in the making, which might require us to put our unique expertise into action. HRT operators are experienced, mature, levelheaded men who function best in the face of a crisis. That is one of the prerequisites identified during HRT selection. Possessing the natural ability to function decisively in the face of a crisis, and having confidence in your training, your equipment, your teammates, and your leadership results in a sense of serenity. Professional athletes possess the same sense of serenity. Gone are the days of nervous jitters. The game becomes a profession. Performing at an exceptional level is expected. Nowhere within the ranks of the HRT will you find the hand-wringing, indecisive pencil dicks typical of FBI management. HRT operators will absolutely react in accordance with what the situation dictates. If that means dropping the hammer, then so be it.

As we neared Anniston, Alabama, there was some question as to whether the C-141 would be able to land at the Municipal Airport. The authorities were not accustomed to having an aircraft of that size setting down at their airport. I didn't worry much about this dilemma, let the Air Force flyboys figure it out. I found a cozy spot on top of some kit bags and lay down. As I stretched out, I mentally inventoried my equipment. J.D. had given each operator on Hotel team a checklist of gear to refer to when packing his individual kit bags, and J.D. made sure this checklist included black socks. J.D. absolutely required everyone on Hotel team to wear tactical black socks. Nothing would set him off quicker than a pair of white gym socks with your assault boots. My gear was intact. Big Jack was next to me swinging in a hammock he had secured between one of the handrails welded to the side of the white mount-out truck and a D-ring he attached to the interior sidewall of the fuselage. Nick was racked out inside the cab of the mount-out truck, and Dave was upfront in the cabin of the aircraft playing cards.

The uniform of the day was the standard military green Nomex flight suit. This was our standard attire throughout any crisis unless we got the command to change into our blacks. If that happened, it signaled we were probably going to conduct an assault. Some of the guys had the tops of their flight suits pulled down with the arms wrapped around their waists. Underneath the flight suit was normally an olive drab or gray T-shirt that had the phrase "H&R Tires and Construction" printed across the front and a drawing of a shovel and mattock with the handles crossing each other. This T-shirt represented the HRT operators' ongoing effort to maintain the shooting house back at Quantico where the Team conducted most of its CQB training. The first generation HRT operators had built the initial shooting house out of tires, four-by-four beams, and gravel, and each subsequent generation of operators maintained it. The H&R Tires and Construction logo was the "unofficial" HRT logo that we could wear in public without anyone knowing what it meant.

The "no-go" logo, on the other hand, is what appears on the official HRT seal. The HRT seal shows a bald eagle descending upon its prey with a broken chain grasped within its talons. The broken chain represents freedom from bondage, oppression, or captors.

Above the eagle is the FBI seal and its motto Fidelity, Bravery, and Integrity. Below the eagle is the HRT motto, which is the Latin phrase *Servare Vitas* (To Save Lives). There were some unofficial patches and T-shirts displaying the no-go logo, but they were kept out of sight of the HRT commander. For whatever reason, the logo was not sanctioned. I suspect having the FBI seal displayed on the logo was the sticking point. Numerous approvals had to be granted by the bean counters at FBIHQ before the FBI seal could be displayed on a unit patch or uniform.

I glanced toward the front of the cabin and saw the head shed in a huddle. They were in contact with the advance and probably had some new intel. Not to worry, we would be receiving an update as soon as we hit the ground. Intelligence briefs would occur periodically. The HRT Two Shop would continue to keep the HRT commander, the assault and sniper supervisors, and the respective TLs up to speed. There is such a thing as information overload, and, as an assaulter, I am interested in only the basics: the facts that directly impact my ability to accomplish the mission. As far as intel goes, some of the information passed is useful, but most is superfluous. In reality, it all boils down to saving the hostage(s) and killing anyone who tries to get in the way. I know that's overly simplistic, but you have to reduce your options to the basics.

The landing at the Anniston Municipal Airport occurred without incident. Guys from the S-4 met us with rental vans and box trucks locked on. Off loading the plane always went quicker than loading it. We distributed equipment between the box trucks, and then lined up the vehicles in preparation for the trip to our prestaging area.

The thirty-mile route between the airport and FCI Talladega was along Talladega County Road 244, a heavily wooded highway typical of the Deep South. As I drove the Hotel team Suburban along the dark highway, following the line of vehicles to our prestaging location, I wondered if General Forrest had made his way along this route in defense of the Confederacy. I rolled down my window and felt the blanket of humid, hot August air. I could make out the shapes of Southern loblolly pines along the edges of the road, and I could smell the distinct aroma of jasmine and gardenia hedgerows as we passed by. The night heat intensified their fragrance. As we drove along Highway 244, I could see the illumination of bright lights on the dark horizon: FCI Talladega. Federal correctional institutions and prisons are not synonymous terms. A prison is a facility that houses prisoners. The criminals or inmates housed within federal correctional institutions, or jails, penitentiaries, penal institutions, hoosegows, lockups, etc. do not deserve to be referred to in the same context or by the same term as prisoners of war. There is nothing synonymous between the two. Inmates are the scourges of society. Prisoners of war are soldiers fighting for a cause.

FCI Talladega is located about forty miles east of Birmingham, Alabama. The facility, which opened in 1979, was designed to house 510 inmates. By March of 1990, the medium-security facility housed 869 inmates. In addition, another 101 inmates were housed at the adjacent minimum-security work farm. Common to most jails around the country, FCI Talladega housed twice the number of inmates its designers had intended. As our conga line approached the front of the facility, I could see the media circus was already on scene. The networks had their large communication vehicles staged with their antennas and satellite dishes raised to broadcast events live as they transpired. Unfortunately, when events slow down, shameless reporters will broadcast fiction if it attracts viewers or sells papers. This is why frequent press briefings are so important. They keep the media informed and reduce the chance of inaccurate reporting. An over zealous media coupled with inaccurate reporting can lead to tragedy and loss of human life. Years later, at the LA Riots,[15] at the Branch Davidian standoff in Waco, Texas, and in Ruby Ridge, Idaho, I would witness examples of the disastrous consequences of an irresponsible media. In each of these instances, the media walked away with blood on its hands, but as always, it's the law enforcement officers who must ultimately respond to public scrutiny.

Jail personnel immediately directed us to drive our vehicles into a sally port. The intent was to get our vehicles inside the secure perimeter of the jail facility before the press figured out what was happening. As it was, there was not much activity among the media ranks. It was late at night and, apparently, things were calm for the moment. This is the norm for a protracted crisis. Unlike two-hour, action-packed movies and television shows where commercials control the clock, there is not something going on continuously during a crisis. In reality, people get hungry and tired. Days, minutes, and hours run together. Time slows down and a routine sets in. This would become increasingly evident within the environment we were about to enter. We drove our vehicles inside the jail perimeter and staged them adjacent to the buildings that housed the jail chapel, weight room, and library. This area would be our home until the crisis was resolved.

Working within the confines of a jail facility was nothing new to me. As a Ventura County Deputy Sheriff, my first thirty-six months with the department were spent working in the jails. Although this was the normal rotation, many of the new deputies got frustrated and impatient. They wanted to get out on the streets. I took a different attitude. Working in the jails gave me the opportunity to observe inmate behavior. I also got to know, by name, every crook in the county of Ventura. No pun intended, I had a captive audience to study. No different from the overcrowded conditions at FCI Talladega, the

Ventura County jails were bursting at the seams. I have never understood why the overcrowding problem isn't resolved by simply building more jails. It's not like there's a shortage of real estate within the United States. We're not talking about beachfront property. Not only does the construction of more jails help eliminate overcrowding, it also creates more steady jobs for the community. I suppose the stigma associated with having a jail in your community factors in to why some communities are resistant, but the problem persists with unemployment ultimately leading to more crime. More crime means more crooks going to jail. More crooks receiving jail sentences means overcrowded conditions and a need for more jails. Then the cycle starts all over again.

One of the most efficient jail facilities I've ever visited is the Louisiana State Penitentiary in Angola, Louisiana. Surrounded by swampland and completely self-sufficient, this facility provides a less-than-inviting environment. The hot, humid, non-air-conditioned cells coupled with long days of physical labor are enough of a deterrent to discourage recidivism. Unfortunately for the inmates at Angola, the average sentence is eighty-plus years. At the Ventura County Sheriff's Department Branch Jail Honor Farm (BJHF), efforts were taken to implement some of the same procedures I witnessed at Angola. Just like Talladega, the BJHF also included medium-and minimum-security facilities. While working at the BJHF, I learned how inmates live and survive while in custody. There is no honor among thieves. Within the custodial environment, inmates will replicate every crime they've committed in open society. This includes rape, murder, assault, arson, mayhem, burglary, robbery, and any other heinous act you can think of. Their crimes are not limited to acts of violence; inmates also commit every white-collar crime they can. Forgery, wire fraud, counterfeiting, receiving and selling stolen property, prostitution, and corruption are just the tip of the iceberg. Inmates, by choice or not, live like animals. The overcrowded conditions contribute to the squalor, but, primarily, inmates live the way they do because that is the environment they know best. I saw it on countless occasions as a cop and a street agent. Suspected criminals and their families living in putrid conditions not as a product of poverty, but, in most cases, because of laziness coupled with drug and alcohol addiction.

It was approaching midnight as we secured the vehicles, but, as always, the HRT hit the ground running. The entire HRT was summoned to meet in a large, open room sparsely furnished with some desks, office chairs, and bookcases against the walls. There were a number of additional metal folding chairs distributed between the ranks. The assault supervisor entered the room and the chatter among the operators diminished. He cleared his throat and in his customary no-nonsense demeanor began. "All right guys, listen up and I'll give you the latest sit-rep." This was military speak for situation report. He had probably been brought up to speed by the S-2 shop and his counterpart from the local SWAT team, who had been temporarily standing in until the HRT arrived on scene.

"First, some good news. The inmates released one hostage, a guard, about an hour after the uprising began. He hurt his neck during the takeover, but he's going to be okay. That leaves us with ten hostages still being held captive in the Alpha Unit. The guard should be able to provide some good intel on what the conditions are like inside, the hostage takers' level of commitment, and what weapons they may have on hand. Apparently, they're moving the hostages around, but at least they're keeping them together…so far. Hopefully, the guard can narrow down the locations where they are holding the other hostages. BOP has a tight perimeter around the building."

Tight perimeter was an understatement. By coincidence, the Bureau of Prisons (BOP) had been training at the facility with a fourteen-member Special Operations Response Team (SORT) at the time of the uprising. They had since brought in further reinforcements and had the Alpha Unit surrounded by a 360-degree perimeter of personnel standing within ten yards of each other. The Alpha Unit is a maximum-security unit within the medium-security correctional facility. In addition to housing the Cuban inmates, inmates with disciplinary problems were also sent to the Alpha Unit. Therefore, the Alpha Unit also consisted of what is referred to as disciplinary segregation. In jailhouse lingo, the Alpha Unit at FCI Talladega was the Hole. Typically, fourteen BOP personnel were assigned to the unit to stand guard over the inmates, who, in this case, included 121 Cuban detainees and 18 Americans in the Hole.

With respect to the hostages, little would be disclosed about who they were. We were given the information about the injured guard and his subsequent release only because it potentially affected our operations and tactics. We made no effort to learn the hostages' names or anything about their personal lives. This is the nature of hostage rescue. Pictures of the hostages were displayed in the CP with their names, a physical description and the agency they belonged to, but beyond that, a degree of anonymity was maintained. This is a necessity. If a hostage goes bad and attempts to assist the terrorists, his or her actions may imperil the other hostages. If this happens then the hostage who "flipped" may have to be neutralized.

Years later, at the crisis at Ruby Ridge, the necessity for this hostage protocol was very apparent. I was tasked with conducting a potential assault in which young girls might attempt to resist rescue and shoot me in the process. The daughters of Randy Weaver had been indoctrinated to hate federal law enforcement. I was mentally prepared to do what was necessary during that crisis to arrest the murderers of U.S. Deputy Marshal William Degan. If these children pointed a gun at me upon entry, I would kill them. Not a situation I was looking forward to, nor a mental decision I enjoyed rehearsing. Despite these children's warped beliefs, they were also considered hostages. I didn't want to know their birthdays or their favorite colors. If I could save them I would, but not if they tried to kill my teammates or me. This was the reality of the crisis and I had a wife and daughter. I would do whatever it took to ensure I went home to them at the end of the day.

The assault supervisor continued, "Our first priority is to get an emergency assault team geared up and in place. TLs, get together with your individual teams and settle in. Some of you remember Atlanta and Oakdale. This is round three and both of those incidents lasted about two weeks a piece. Golf team, you're up first. Hotel, you relieve them at 0600." In the event of an emergency requiring an immediate tactical response, the team on standby would get the ticket. An emergency assault plan (EAP) had already been drafted and sent up the chain of command for approval. The operators of the standby team were required to fully jock up and be ready to respond at a moment's notice. They would position their assault vehicle next to the staging area, and one operator would stay behind the wheel throughout the shift, prepared to deliver his teammates to the breach point if necessary.

The assault supervisor concluded the brief by stating, "Listen guys, make no mistake, these inmates are dangerous. Most of them are HIV positive, and they have a one-way ticket back to Cuba looking them in the face. This is their last opportunity to try to prevent deportation. Castro won't have a welcome party to greet them at the airport. In fact, they'll probably never make it off the tarmac alive. TLs, I'll see you in the morning at 0630. I'll have a draft deliberate assault plan (DAP) ready by then." With that, the meeting adjourned.

Hotel team didn't get the first shift as the emergency assault team, but we were on deck. This had J.D. at a medium hover again. He called Hotel together to issue marching orders. Hotel team mustered in the corner of the same open office space. Other assault and sniper teams were also meeting in other parts of the room. J.D.'s first concern was Hotel team's readiness for the morning shift as the emergency assault team. His first words were, "I want everybody to get his ready bag and stage them in this corner. Then lay your gear out, so it's good to go in the morning. We'll relieve Golf team at 0545 hours." J.D. always liked to show up early when relieving another team. That way there was ample time for a brief-back from the team going off shift, and it was a courteous precedent to set for the other teams.

J.D. continued, "We'll go with green flight suits, standard assault gear, and ballistic helmets. Our primary weapon will be the MP5. Go ahead and carry one of your Browning Hi-Powers in your holster rig. Holster the second Browning on your chest."

Standard assault gear includes Level III body armor that inserts into a black body armor carrier. The carrier slips over your head and then fastens beneath your arms. Two, three-inch-wide Velcro straps then wrap around your chest and above your waist to further secure the carrier in place. The ballistic Kevlar inserts fit so they overlap on each side of your torso. More than one cop has died while wearing body armor because the ballistic vest didn't come together on the sides. It always amazes me that a cop can get shot and die from a bullet that finds the path to that one vulnerable location. A crook, on the other hand, can get shot twice with a slug from a shotgun and be out of the hospital in two days with injuries that are no more than a nuisance. I know this from personal experience. Remember my partner, the Z-man? He blasted a fugitive with two slugs from a shotgun, and the guy absorbed the rounds like he was shot by a BB gun. In addition to the ballistic inserts, the body armor carrier also has a sleeve located over the chest where a ceramic plate is inserted. The ceramic plate provides ballistic protection for rifled caliber rounds up to and including .223. The Level III ballistic protection only stops handgun caliber rounds up to and including 9mm.

Numerous other accessories are also placed on the front outside of the carrier. A handcuff carrier holds a set of rigid anodized black handcuffs. Magazine pouches hold an assortment of magazines for both the primary shoulder weapon and the handguns. A knife and sheath are secured on the three-inch Velcro strap that wraps around the waist. A holster affixed over your chest houses a second Browning Hi-Power 9mm, single action, semi-automatic pistol. The position where this weapon is carried becomes important when a crisis site involves close confines. Operators can't risk getting hung up during movement because they're carrying a pistol in a holster slung from their hip.

Hanging from the front of the body armor carrier is a Level III ballistic flap designed to protect the respective operator's groin area. Affectionately referred to as the "pecker pad," this piece of ballistic protection has a pocket for stowing miscellaneous items. I normally carry some extra flex-cuffs, a small notebook and pen for jotting down subject descriptions, addresses, and suspected weapons or any other relevant pieces of information (remember HRT operators are FBI special agents first and foremost), and some chemical light sticks. Chemical light sticks are six-inch plastic tubes filled with two chemicals that react when the tube is bent and the chemicals are mixed. The resulting chemical reaction provides a fluorescent light source. The low-light illumination comes in handy for reading a map, looking into a dark elevator shaft, or marking a location.

The back of the body armor carrier accommodates even more accessories. A pouch holds the individual operator's radio. Another pouch adjacent to the radio pouch is designed to hold a bailout bottle. The bailout bottle, similar in shape to a scuba tank but much smaller, provides the operator with approximately ten minutes of positive pressure compressed air in the event of a fire or toxic gas contamination. Another pouch that hangs from the back of the body armor carrier holds a gas mask. The gas mask can be removed from the pouch and used independently with a filter, or the gas mask can be attached to a hose that leads to the bailout bottle. Four more pockets hold flash-bang or concussion grenades. These pockets are situated so the operator behind you in the line of march can reach forward and pluck a "bang" from his fellow operator's back to throw before entering a room.

With the conglomeration of attached equipment on the body armor carrier, it totals out to weigh about fifty pounds. This combined with the weight of the fully loaded MP5 submachine gun, ballistic helmet, and tactical gun belt bumps the overall weight to about seventy-five pounds. This is the standard load-out no matter what your body size. With a standard body weight of 210 pounds, when I enter the door of a crisis site I'm pushing 285 pounds. As the point man, I need to be quick on my feet, so I carry only what is absolutely essential to my job. This is unlike the breachers who follow in the line of march and are loaded down with all of the additional breaching gear. This adds another fifty plus pounds based upon what type of doors may be encountered. There is a fundamental need for above-average upper body strength, and HRT selection includes numerous "load-bearing" evolutions designed to test this required capability. Falling off a fast rope or not being able to keep up the pace because you can't handle the weight is unforgiving. The results are tragic. To date, political correctness, aimed at reducing physical requirements from job selection criteria, has not been forced upon the counterterrorism team community, but, have no doubt, the ivory towers that harbor the liberal agenda are working hard to "correct" this perceived abomination.

J.D. continued with his marching orders. "Scar, make sure the Hotel Suburban is ready to go in the event of an emergency assault." I knew the line of vehicles had stopped en route to the jail and topped off the gas tanks. I also knew all of the gear from inside the vehicle had been off-loaded. The only thing left to do was to rig the roof platform with two emergency assault ladders. With Corderman's help, I could knock that out in fifteen minutes.

J.D. then turned to the two Hotel team breachers and told them to make sure they had some explosive charges and the appropriate mechanical breaching equipment ready to go in the morning in case an emergency assault was ordered. This would require the two breachers to build some slap shots powerful enough to blow a locked office door. They would also need to break out the circular saws, the cutting torch, bolt cutters, rams, and sledgehammers, all pieces of breaching gear that might be needed during an emergency assault. J.D. told the Hotel team EMT, who was also the HRT paramedic, to get the ambulance staged and ready for an emergency medevac if necessary.

An emergency assault is a shit sandwich. If it happens, then it means hostages have been (or are being) seriously injured or murdered. It requires the assault team to respond to the actions of the hostage takers without the control and precision that are part of a deliberate assault. In an emergency assault, the hostage takers are partially in control and are manipulating the actions of the assault team. A deliberate assault, on the other hand, occurs at the choosing of the on-scene commander (OSC). If the OSC determines the situation is deteriorating and negotiations are no longer a viable option, then a deliberate assault can be executed. This option gives the assault team the advantage of rehearsing and meticulously striving to ensure that those fundamentally important components of CQB (speed, surprise, violence of action, and a fail-safe breach) are foolproof.

As the Hotel team meeting ended, J.D. asked the assistant team leader (ATL) to make sure each Hotel team member had a place to rack out. Military cots were available. Hotel team would muster again at 0530 prepared to relieve Golf team. Corderman and I broke off to take care of the Hotel Suburban, then we picked up two cots. We set the cots up in a small office adjacent to the meeting room. The office normally belonged to the jail chaplain, but Dave and I would be sharing it for the duration of the mission. I unrolled and blew up the inflatable pad I carried with my kit bag, then laid it on the cot and covered it with a woodland camo poncho liner. I stuffed one of my waterproof bags with some socks for a pillow. Dave was going through the same routine. I undressed and lay down on the cot. Dave cut the lights. I checked my G-Shock wristwatch with the illumination function. The time was 0220. Two hours of sleep then rise and shine. I knew we had it better than the hostages.

I've never needed an alarm clock and I don't drink coffee. I've always had an internal clock that wakes me up no matter how long I've been asleep and no matter what time I'm scheduled to awake. At 0500 I rolled out of bed. Day two of the uprising was underway. Several cases of MREs were stacked outside the door of our sleeping area. I had lived for weeks on the predecessor to

MREs—C rations—when I was with the U.S. Forest Service. Some scrambled eggs, peach slices in water, and the nut cake were all I needed to start the morning. MREs even have a small bottle of Tabasco sauce included to spice up the cuisine. Some of the operators would consume MREs whenever the HRT was deployed just so they could pocket the per diem. I've never known anyone who got wealthy saving his per diem. After eating breakfast, I grabbed a paper bath towel and headed toward the portable shower facilities that had been set up behind the building where we were staged. A hot shower goes a long way in terms of getting the body stimulated. Still, drying off with a paper bath towel is like drying off with notebook paper—not very absorbent. Along with paper bath towels, there were paper sleeping bags. Sleeping in a paper sleeping bag gives you a firsthand experience of what sleeping on a park bench with newspapers for sheets must feel like. I had slept in my black Patagonia shorts and an olive drab T-shirt. After a quick shit, shower, and shave I put my shorts and T-shirt back on and then put on my green flight suit. I put on black socks over a pair of white cotton socks and then my black GSG9 assault boots. Dave was already up and dressed. Dave, like many operators in the CT world, never wore underwear. In fact, he was always in the buff under his flight suit. Maybe the ventilation is better?

At 0545 we linked up with Golf team and received a brief on what had occurred during their shift. The Golf TL provided more details regarding the events that had led to the uprising, some of which had been passed from the hostage who had been previously released. The takeover had occurred the day before 32 of the jail's 121 Cuban inmates were to be deported to their homeland. Some of these inmates were among the one hundred detainees who had been transferred to FCI Talladega from Atlanta and Oakdale in 1987 after the uprisings that had occurred at each of those facilities. After the 1987 uprisings, FCI Talladega had become the final stop for hundreds of additional inmates destined for deportation to Cuba.

On Wednesday morning, the guard, a rookie, had taken thirty-five Cuban inmates out of their cells and handcuffed them prior to escorting them to the showers and recreation area. Once there, the guard began the process of removing the handcuffs. First, he reached through an eighteen-by-sixteen-inch window, then, one-by-one, each inmate backed up to the window and the guard removed the handcuffs. This was the daily routine inside the jail, and it was during this time that the inmates succeeded in overpowering the guard and gaining control of the Alpha Unit. Two inmates had approached the door to the exercise area and reached through the bars to grab the rookie guard. The inmates then pulled the guard up to the door, took his handcuffs and cuffed him. They took his keys, freed themselves, and then released eighty-seven other inmates. The inmates dragged the guard to the door of the facility designated as A-Wing and forced him to ask the four guards inside the wing to open the door. When the guards opened the door, the inmates stormed in and immediately overpowered them. The inmates handcuffed each of these guards and then began releasing more inmates from their cells. The noise had alerted the guards in B-Wing, and, looking through a window into A-Wing, they saw the inmates in control. Ultimately, B-Wing was evacuated and the inmates took complete control of the entire Alpha Unit.

Initially, the inmates were armed with handmade knives and other sharp instruments, but now they would have access to other weapons including batons and possibly Mace or pepper spray. As with most jail facilities around the country, the guards and jail employees inside the facility do not carry firearms. I knew from personal experience that carrying a firearm inside a jail facility was foolish. Many times while working in the Ventura County jails, I stood inside the units among several hundred inmates. If the inmates had wanted to take me hostage or kill me on the spot, having a gun would have made little difference. The reality is you're at the mercy of the inmates once you enter their environment. You become part of the food chain. The only thing that keeps an inmate from risking an attack is the understanding that serious repercussions will result. But, as with the situation we were facing at Talladega, sometimes the risk outweighs the repercussions.

As of Thursday, the inmates continued to hold ten hostages. The hostages included three women and seven men. Six of the hostages were guards, three were Immigration and Naturalization Service employees, and one was the facility secretary. That same day, one of the Cuban inmates identified himself as Jesus De Armas while talking to a reporter for Miami's Spanish-language *El Nuevo Herald* via telephone. He claimed to be the leader of the uprising and told the reporter, "We're willing to kill everyone to not go to Cuba. The thing here is limited to three words, *freedom or death*." The inmates and hostages continued to be contained within the Alpha Unit. The inmates could not gain access to the outside perimeter of the housing unit because they didn't have those keys.

The Golf TL told us the inmates and the hostages had not been fed since the uprising. I knew this could become a problem for the hostages. The inmates, on the other hand, would have access to the abundance of snacks they purchase through the jailhouse commissary or canteen. I had witnessed this process firsthand: the hardcore career criminals would intimidate the young inmates and either force them to buy certain items (usually cigarettes, coffee, and high-calorie junk food) or they would just steal whatever the young inmates had purchased. The high-sugar content snacks are desirable to the junkies who need the sweets to offset their craving for drugs while they're incarcerated. This is another example of the jailhouse food chain that exists on the inside. Young, naive inmates are the main prey for the institutionalized career criminal/predator.

Hotel team assumed the shift, and Golf team headed toward their racks. Dave and I went outside and climbed into the Hotel team Suburban. I turned toward Dave and said, "Dave, I know how these inmates think. They're predators, and now they have access to a new prey in the form of ten hostages."

"I know, Jim. At Atlanta, they had 124 hostages and at Oakdale they had 28. It was easier to get lost in the crowd for those folks. I'm really worried about the women this time."

Dave's comment reminded me that "getting lost in the crowd" inside a jail is not easy, and that's why so many inmates join gangs for protection. I remembered the Penitentiary of New Mexico riots, which had occurred at the Santa Fe facility in 1980. That uprising is considered one of the most brutal on record. During that crisis, the inmates raped, sodomized, and murdered at will. In one instance, they drove a metal stake through the head of another inmate who was being held in protective custody and believed to be a jailhouse informant. It seemed no one got lost in the crowd during the Penitentiary of New Mexico crisis.

To complicate matters, avoiding the other inmates doesn't necessarily mean you're going to escape the attention of law enforcement. While assigned to the Albuquerque Division, one of my first cases was an 88A-Unlawful Flight to Avoid Confinement (UFAC) fugitive matter. That is bureau speak that basically means a federal warrant was issued for an individual who escaped from jail or never showed up to go to jail after being sentenced and was presumed to have crossed the state line. In this case, the individual was John Cameron Mygatt, who was wanted for escaping from the Penitentiary of New Mexico in Santa Fe. Mygatt was convicted of kidnapping the wife of a prominent Albuquerque doctor and holding her for ransom in a remote cabin located in the mountains east of the city. Fortunately, the victim escaped by getting her hands on a bar of soap left in the cabin. She used the soap and her saliva as a lubricant on her wrists and slipped out of the cuffs while Mygatt was off negotiating for the ransom. Mygatt actually got away with the ransom, but was later captured in California. After being sentenced to the Penitentiary of New Mexico, he survived the infamous Penitentiary of New Mexico riots and eventually escaped. At the time of the escape, the jail administration had assigned Mygatt as a "trustee." In other words, he was allowed to assist the jail staff with janitorial duties and had supervised access to secure areas like administrative office space. I've always had a problem with this term. No inmate can be trusted. It should be noted that many times "trustees" are also jailhouse informants.

When I inherited the case, Mygatt had been a fugitive for several years. Tenacity and dogged determination are the keys to success in this type of investigation. In addition, I believe that the victims of heinous crimes deserve vindication. In other words, the scumbags should serve their prescribed sentences. I immediately located Mygatt's family in Albuquerque and eventually learned that Mygatt also had family in Virginia. I contacted the FBI office in Richmond, Virginia, and gave them an address. Agents from Richmond, accompanied by local law enforcement authorities, paid the address a visit one foggy evening. When they entered the front door, John Cameron Mygatt ran out the back door. One of the local cops gave chase. During the foot pursuit, Mygatt apparently couldn't see very well due to the fog and accidentally ran over the side of a cliff. Unfortunately the cop who was in pursuit of him also plunged over the precipice. Lucky for the cop, Mygatt broke his fall. Mygatt, on the other hand, was not so lucky. The fall combined with the cop landing on him snapped his back. Mygatt was subsequently extradited to New Mexico in traction. He was returned to the Penitentiary of New Mexico to finish his sentence. The same institution where inmates suspected of being informants have metal spikes driven through their heads. Sometimes justice is served.

I wasn't sure if justice would be served this time around. The 0600-1400 shift passed without incident. Dave and I spent most of the time in the Suburban. We switched off occasionally to go and get a drink or hit the head. The negotiations with the inmates were ongoing. The demand remained the same, "Freedom in the United States rather than deportation to Cuba." Spanish-speaking negotiators were on scene as well as the SACs from Birmingham, Knoxville, Miami, and Philadelphia. At 1345, Echo team showed up to assume their shift. J.D. briefed the Echo TL and we turned the emergency assault team responsibilities over to the Echo team assaulters. Dave and I stowed our gear by our ready bags. We kept our green flight suits on and headed toward the chow hall. The jail cafeteria was up and running.

The HRT was staged inside the jail perimeter and out of sight of the Alpha Unit. When we walked to the chow hall, we became exposed to the front of the Alpha Unit. The inmates kept sentries posted at the windows. We always took precaution not to walk to the cafeteria in a large group. We would move in pairs so the inmates didn't get alarmed and think an assault force was preparing to conduct a rescue of the hostages. Within the jail environment, the walls have ears. This is a given. The authorities listen to and monitor everything the inmates do, and the inmates do the same thing to the authorities through their own network of trustees. Like I stated earlier, trustees can't be trusted. They are the eyes and ears of the inmate population. As Dave and I walked to the chow hall, I could feel inmate eyes watching our every move. The entire facility was in lockdown, meaning that every inmate was confined to his cell in the other four units within FCI Talladega.

Dave and I entered the cafeteria and grabbed a tray. As we moved through the chow line, I loaded my plate with fried chicken and rice. As we took a seat at the long table, I felt like I was in grade school again. Several other Hotel team members and some guys from the sniper side of the house were also seated at the table. Given that we were staged inside a secure jail facility, this deployment had a limited sniper mission. Although a couple of sniper/observer teams, who would be posted on the rooftops adjacent to the Alpha Unit, would report to the Sniper Tactical Operations Center (S-TOC) any observed activity, the sniper teams during this mission would function primarily as assaulters in the event we "went in." This is why snipers cross-train as assaulters. This time instead of lying in the weeds and covering our backs, the snipers would get an opportunity to rescue some hostages and put the *habeas grabbus* on the scumbags responsible for the crime.

I've never been known as a picky eater. My time eating at college training tables, in fire camps and in the Ventura County jails taught me to consume in abundance. I finished my first plate of food and started to go for seconds. Corderman looked at me and asked, "Scar, where you going?"

"Where do you think? I'm carbo loading."

"Why don't you finish eating what's in your hair?"

I looked at my reflection in the window and noticed I had a

bunch of rice stuck in my flat top. The guys got a kick out of this. Scarhead with kernels of rice shish kebabed to his hair. I brushed the rice out of my hair and headed to the chow line for seconds. As I walked away, I turned to Dave and said, "I love it here!"

After chow, we left in pairs and walked back to the staging area. I browsed through the books stacked on the bookshelf inside the office where Dave and I had our hooch set up. I found a book titled *Fort Laramie and the Sioux* by Remi Nadeau. They were a defiant band of warriors. I lay down on my cot and began to read.

With the aid of a pair of squeezable Styrofoam earplugs, I slept soundly for several hours. When I awoke, I removed the earplugs, sat up, and put on my running shoes. I then headed for the jailhouse weight room. Inmates place a lot of status on being buffed. I've always thought it was a contradiction when the inmate, who has been convicted and sentenced to jail for a crime, has access to a fully equipped workout facility at his or her disposal while incarcerated. But hey, inmates have rights too. Well, now I had the right to use their weight room until this crisis ended. The weight room was conveniently located in the same building immediately adjacent to where the HRT was staged. We're not talking state-of-the-art machines, but it had all the requisite equipment needed for a good workout. The antiquated 1950s vintage dumbbells and narrow bar fixed-weight barbells were good enough—this was the type of equipment I started training with back when I was fourteen-years-old. No treadmills, Stairmasters, or stationary bikes were available, but I always carry a jump rope with me. This took care of the cardiovascular part of the workout. In addition, Nick, Dave, and I set up a running route inside the jail's industry warehouse. This was where inmates worked to produce manufactured goods. At FCI Talladega, they didn't manufacture license plates, but they did make brooms in all shapes and sizes. We set up a "grinder" course that included sit-ups, push-ups, dips, and pull-ups. The warehouse was not air-conditioned. Big ventilation fans kept the air moving. A one-hour grinder was sufficient to get the blood flowing and break a good sweat.

After the workout, it was back to the shower and then time for dinner at the chow hall. As Dave and I headed back for another meal, I thought about how quickly I had slipped into the institutional routine. This cycle would continue until the negotiators resolved the crisis or the inmates did something that required a tactical resolution. Until then, our marching orders were explicit: Hurry up and wait.

File No.: Chapter Six
Subject: Prep Time

As day three of the crisis began, I finished reading about the exploits of Crazy Horse. His relentless attempt to resist the white man was futile. The westward expansion of the United States was inevitable. Crazy Horse, along with his peers, was forced to react out of desperation. The policy of the U.S. government did not adequately take into account the plight the Sioux Nation faced. As a nomadic tribe of warriors and hunters, the Sioux did not easily conform to the rigors of reservation life. Treaties were signed and promises were made, but ultimately the issue facing the Sioux would be resolved only through violent conflict. The day would come when either the Sioux Nation would surrender and accept its "new" life in the confines of the reservation, or it would be physically forced to accept this eventuality. Compromise, negotiations, and deliberations would cease and the Sioux Indian would either succumb to the will of the United States or die. Crazy Horse realized either choice meant an end to the Sioux Nation, so he opted for defiance.

At 0500 hours, the ATL for Hotel team stuck his head in the door and told Dave and me to get chow and to be ready to go back on emergency assault duty by 0545. Not a problem, even though it had been passed to us the day before that the two HRT sniper teams were going to be included in the rotation for emergency assault duty. This should have meant that our team's shift would come up every other day. Apparently, this hadn't been worked out yet.

As I got up and put on my flight suit, I noticed the distinct smell of the jailhouse environment. It reminded me of soiled linens. A smell I had become all too familiar with during high school when I drove the route for National Linen Service between Pensacola Beach and Fort Walton Beach, Florida, as a summer job. The sour smell underscored the spoiled lives of inmates sentenced to FCI Talladega. Dave was up and dressed. We both headed back to the chow hall for breakfast. Eat, pull our emergency assault shift, eat lunch, work out, eat dinner, work out, and then back in the rack. This was the routine so far. As we moved through the chow line, I loaded my plate with French toast. French toast, served everywhere, is a staple of the institutional environment. The Ventura County jails served it, the inmates who were brought in to staff the chow lines served it in the fire camps, and now FCI Talladega served it. The availability of French toast for breakfast symbolized to me a constant. In other words, French toast is and always will be available at breakfast despite the uncertainties associated with the crisis at hand.

With our bellies full of French toast and bacon, Dave and I headed back to the staging area. There we met up with the rest of Hotel team and put on our assault gear prior to relieving Charlie team, which had worked the night shift this time instead of Golf team. The HRT consists of two sections: Hotel and Echo assault teams belong to the Blue section; Charlie and Golf assault teams belong to Gold section. The snipers support either the Blue or Gold section as needed. The Charlie TL passed to J.D. the most recent written intel report that the Two Shop had compiled. J.D. called Hotel team together and brought us up to speed on some of the highlights included in the written report. Then J.D. passed the report around to give each operator a chance to read the details for himself. The rioting Cuban inmates were among the 125,000 Cuban refugees who came to the United States in the 1980 Mariel boatlift. Most of the Cuban refugees eventually merged into American society, but the Immigration and Naturalization Service (INS) detained those who were mental patients or criminals released from Cuban jails. In addition, after their arrival to the United States, if any of the Cubans committed crimes, they were detained by the INS after completing their prescribed sentences.

By 1984, the INS had identified 2,746 detained Cubans as people they wanted deported back to Cuba. Of this number, 201 Cubans were deported, but the relationship with Cuba deteriorated and deportations ceased until 1987. At this time there were 3,800 Cuban detainees remaining from the Mariel boatlift. Of this number, 2,500 of the Cuban detainees had been in INS custody since 1980. The federal courts ruled that as non-U.S. citizens, the Cubans were subject to, not a trial, but to indefinite detention and deportation pursuant to INS administrative procedures. This ruling, criticized by the Cubans as unfair, led to the 1987 riots in Atlanta and Oakdale, which resulted in a total of 152 hostages taken and $50 million in damage. The report revealed that among the 121 Cuban inmates housed in the Alpha Unit, 11 were involved in the Atlanta uprising and 20 at the Oakdale incident.

The 1987 takeovers were resolved eventually through negotiations. Part of the negotiated resolution included a reform of the process for reviewing the status of Mariel boatlift Cubans who had violated the law once in the United States. Also, a second appeals procedure was added to the INS hearing process, which determined whether a detained and jailed Mariel boatlift Cuban should be paroled into U.S. society. The new procedure resulted in more than 1,800 Mariel boatlift Cuban detainees, originally on the list of those to be deported, being subsequently paroled into society. Once paroled, 270 of them violated the law and were sent back to jail. These

Cuban inmates would once again be subject to deportation when they completed their sentences.

Of the approximately 800 Cuban detainees who did not qualify for parole, 457 were deported back to Cuba. In addition, 45 died while in custody and 225 remained in custody at over seventy federal, state, and local jails. Fifty out of the 225 were approved for parole and were waiting for sponsorship before they could be released into a halfway house. This left 175 original Mariel boatlift Cuban detainees who had exhausted all appeals and were subject to deportation to Cuba. The 121 Cuban inmates at FCI Talladega were among this group, and their situation was desperate.

FCI Talladega environment was designed to provide all of the essential security requirements and standard operating procedures to house society's failures. Sadly, those failures often extend beyond the individual criminal who has been convicted and sentenced for crimes against society. In this instance, the failure was the inability to effectively legislate U.S. immigration procedures largely due to flawed international diplomacy and bureaucratic incompetence. For the detained Cubans, the options were bleak: a trip back to Cuba meant a potential death sentence, but remaining in the United States meant indefinite incarceration. The report described the Cubans as tense and volatile. Like the Sioux Indians when faced with a life sentence on the reservation, the Cuban inmates had chosen defiance.

After reading the report, J.D. handed out shift assignments. Dave and I would handle the first few hours of the standby emergency assault duty shift. We both climbed into the prestaged Suburban and waited. In the event an emergency assault was needed, we would be at the ready. As we sat there, negotiations between Gary, the head negotiator, and the inmates were ongoing. Although several negotiators would be used throughout the standoff, Gary, to his credit, had successfully resolved numerous standoffs in the past. He had also worked closely with the HRT on several past occasions. Sensitive to the needs of the tactical element, Gary would strive to extract relevant information from the hostage takers—information that could potentially assist with planning an assault. Gary had a reassuring manner with those he negotiated with, and when he combined it with the negotiation tactic of active listening,[16] he could slowly lull the hostage takers into believing that he actually understood why it was necessary to take hostages and risk the lives of innocent people.

Through previous negotiations, Gary got the inmates to allow "pill call" to be conducted at the front door to the Alpha Unit. During pill call, the inmates had presented the medical personnel with a written message demanding that an Atlanta-based attorney by the name of Gary Leshaw be allowed to represent them. Apparently, Mr. Leshaw had represented many other Cuban detainees who, it was determined, were ineligible for U.S. citizenship and subject to deportation. In addition to Mr. Leshaw, the inmates also demanded that *El Nuevo Herald* reporter Cynthia Corzo and CNN reporter Brian Campbell be made available to them in order to broadcast their plight and their demands.

At the time of the FCI Talladega hostage crisis, I was not a trained hostage negotiator. I later went through the FBI's Hostage Negotiations School to better understand the negotiation process. From a tactical perspective, it's very important to understand what information the negotiators are extracting and why the negotiators are proceeding in a certain direction. It also helps when negotiators are educated in terms of what information may be vital to planning a tactical assault. This could include the number of hostage takers, the number and condition of hostages, where both parties are located inside the crisis site, the availability and type of weapons, etc. I know

now that introducing third-party intermediaries[17] is not a preferred negotiation tactic. Having a third party in the mix who is talking directly to the hostage takers is hard to control. It interferes with the negotiation tactic of mentally fatiguing the hostage takers with a roller-coaster ride of protracted conversation. It's not that using third-party intermediaries doesn't work sometimes, it's that using them can also be disastrous. The Branch Davidian standoff in Waco, Texas, is an example of how third-party intermediaries can offer nothing but prolonged frustration. During this crisis, David Koresh used various third-party attorneys as a stall tactic to manipulate the authorities. All the while, he was moving forward with his plan for mass suicide and murder. The third-party intermediaries did nothing but provide him more time to prepare. My experience tells me that when third-party intermediaries begin to be considered as an option by the negotiators, it's because all other options have failed. As I've told more than one negotiator, "The best thing a negotiator can do is convince the hostage taker to look out the window; a sniper will do the rest."

The agreement between the inmates and the negotiators regarding "pill call" contributed significantly to the ability to derive intelligence about what was going on inside the Alpha Unit. Each time medical personnel made a sick call visit, they were able to inquire about, and on occasion see firsthand, the condition of the hostages. It was suspected that the hostages were surviving with little or no food. The inmates were also monitored for malnutrition. The food available to the inmates was known to be primarily junk food obtained from the inmate commissary. Eventually this diet would take its toll on the inmates. The medical personnel who conducted the "pill call" included legitimate medical doctors. Also dressed in a white MD jacket was an operator from Hotel team who was the Team paramedic. During each visit, he made mental notes regarding the well-being of the hostages and the inmates. His intelligence report, given to the HRT commander, would include any observed injuries and his estimation of the psychological state of the inmates and hostages. In other words, he would try to assess if the hostages had succumbed to the Stockholm Syndrome. In addition, he would try to determine who among the inmates was visually in charge. All of this information would be passed to the negotiators for possible confirmation and to the tactical team for inclusion in the assault plans as applicable.

Each time the medical personnel moved forward for a sick call, a security element consisting of two armed HRT operators moved forward with them to provide protection in the event the inmates tried to assault or take the medical personnel hostage as well. One of the HRT operators assigned this responsibility was Ray, a Golf team member who I had become good friends with during our time together on the Team. Ray was a native of Rhode Island and had spent many summers employed as a lifeguard on the beaches in his home state. He was a superb athlete and had been the referee during my rock 'em, sock 'em boxing match with Big Jack. During a training evolution at Quantico, Ray and I were among a group of operators tasked with jumping from the skids of a helicopter into Lake Lunga as an insertion technique. This technique is referred to as helocasting. Each time we boarded the aircraft and positioned ourselves on the skids, the pilot would ask, "How fast and how high?" Of course, we would always say, "Five knots faster and ten feet higher than the last run." As we took off this time, I saw Ray through the open doors of the aircraft standing on the opposite skid. As we made our approach to the lake, I could see the pilot was beginning to level off at about thirty-five feet. This is pretty high for a helocast, especially when you combine the height with the forward momentum of approximately twenty-five knots. Another operator was standing beside me. On his side of the bird, another operator stood beside Ray. The pilot gave us the signal and three of us jumped. As the bird was pulling away and gaining altitude, I saw Ray standing on the skid. At approximately sixty feet, he jumped. Of course, his speed by then was probably approaching forty knots. He hit the water surface and bounced. I immediately swam over to him. He was out cold. We dragged him to the shore, and he slowly came around. We assured him that he had the record for the day, never mind the fact that he damn near drowned and was ultimately diagnosed with a bruised heart from the impact. That's what I liked about Ray. His willingness to push the envelope.

As Ray and the other operator moved forward with the medical personnel, Ray was tasked with collecting any information that could be relevant to a tactical resolution. He looked for any weapons displayed by the inmates as well as details about the front entry. He noted the construction of the doors, the direction the doors opened, the type of doorknobs and locks, the presence of any windows and the material they were made of (glass, Lexan, wire mesh, etc.), and if the openings included steel bars. Much of this information was available on the floor plans for the facility, but it had to be confirmed. The sniper/observers would try to gather this information by looking through their optics, but some areas were out of their view. Ray also made note of any additional barricades or obstructions the inmates may have put in place. It was noted the doors had been subsequently handcuffed closed. The inmates had cuffed two doors together from the inside. This information would potentially become a factor when it came time to determine what breaching techniques we would utilize.

As well as an opportunity to observe and collect information, the sick call also provided an opportunity to insert monitoring devices into the facility. The hostage takers should presume that anytime anything is passed to the inmates it has the potential to provide listening and/or visual monitoring capability. The tech agents can insert a microphone just about anywhere. Many times the hostage takers during a crisis are well aware that anything they receive from the FBI probably has a monitoring device included. The thing is, they normally can't find it. FBI special agent electronic technicians (ETs) work miracles in this arena. As I mentioned previously, the walls have ears. There is no expectation of privacy inside a penal institution. The legal "experts" were more than a little concerned about whether to obtain an emergency wiretap warrant through the Title III legislation, which provides law enforcement with wire tapping authority if probable cause can be shown to support the need. Both the obvious danger that existed for the hostages and the standard jail security policy, which precludes any expectation of privacy, were enough to justify non-consensual monitoring of the inmates. Nevertheless as a precaution in the world of civil lawsuits and unscrupulous defense attorneys, a warrant was applied for and obtained.

The HRT commander and the assault supervisor entered the room where we were gathered for an early morning full-Team briefing. The assault supervisor took the floor with his standard no-bullshit demeanor. "All right, guys, listen up. We're entering day four of this crisis. So far, the word is that the hostages remain unharmed. The frequent sick calls and negotiations with the inmates support this. Apparently, the media is monitoring some of the negotiations."

This was not uncommon; the media frequently eavesdrops on law enforcement radio communications with scanners and shared non-secure frequencies. Initially, the negotiators and inmates had communicated over walkie-talkies that the inmates had taken from the hostages. In addition, the inmates, who were aware the media could monitor their broadcasts, intentionally tried to contact the media, via the same walkie-talkies, in an effort to sway public opinion.

"To address this problem, the ETs have jammed the frequencies the media are monitoring. The negotiators are also restricting their conversations with the inmates to more secure telephone lines."

Public exposure of the negotiations by the media can compromise the safety of the hostages. In this instance, the media was receiving only one side of the conversation. The inmates' side. Filling in the blanks, which the media is known for doing, would provide a distorted account to the public regarding what the conditions were really like inside the Alpha Unit, and potentially diminish, in the eyes of the public, the danger the hostages truly faced.

"As most of you know, the rest of the inmates housed here at FCI Talladega are in twenty-four-hour lockdown. This is beginning to cause some concern to the warden, so efforts are under way to move the majority of these inmates to other facilities over the next couple of days. This works to our advantage because tomorrow evening at 1900 hours we will begin rehearsing our deliberate assault plan (DAP) in Bravo Unit, one of the adjacent housing units here at FCI Talladega. Most of the inmates should be out of that facility by then. The ones who haven't been relocated will be confined to their cells and the windows in their cell doors will be shielded so they can't watch our movements.

"Currently the negotiators have not been able to determine which inmate is calling the shots. It seems like there's a struggle for control. This is probably not a good thing for the hostages. Some of the inmates are extremely violent and could see the lack of leadership as an opportunity to harm the hostages. Gentlemen, if it looks like this is going to happen, we're going in. So stay alert. TLs get with me and I'll provide a copy of the DAP for you to share with your team."

The meeting broke up, and Hotel team headed for our next emergency assault shift. Before Dave and I climbed back into the prestaged Suburban, we walked around to the side of the building so we could get a visual of the front of Alpha Unit. I also wanted to see where the Bravo Unit was located in relationship to the crisis site. I noticed the BOP SORT personnel who surrounded the perimeter of Alpha Unit had each taken a couple steps toward the crisis site, thus reducing the distance between them and the building. This was one of those small, subtle maneuvers that law enforcement officers deployed to taunt the criminal(s). The negotiators were probably unaware this was happening. The BOP SORT personnel were frustrated—they would be the ones who would eventually have to clean up this mess. It didn't matter if the situation was resolved through negotiations or a tactical assault, the BOP personnel would ultimately be responsible for housing the inmates when the crisis was over and then returning to work in the same conditions that existed before the takeover. The BOP knew some of their own were being held hostage, so this methodical movement closer was a message to the inmates that the time was coming.

Day five began when I awoke from a dream about my wife and baby daughter whom I had not been able to contact since arriving at FCI Talladega. My wife would have to monitor the crisis through the news and her close network of other HRT wives. The wives, which included Louise Corderman, talked and met frequently while the Team was on the road. I rolled out of bed and began to prepare for the next shift. Dave was up and moving around. We both got dressed and headed for chow and some more of our favorite breakfast, French toast. As we walked to the cafeteria, I glanced over at Bravo Unit. We would begin our rehearsals there tonight at 1900 hours.

After breakfast, Dave and I headed toward the emergency assault staging area. During the brief prior to assuming emergency assault responsibilities, we learned that 150 inmates had been transferred during the night to another jail facility. This left 812 inmates still in lockdown at FCI Talladega including the 121 inmates in Alpha Unit. In addition, 164 inmates were confined to their cells at an adjacent minimum-security facility.

During the shift, negotiators continued to talk to the inmates. When medical personnel attempted to conduct a sick call, the inmates placed a blanket over the Alpha Unit door and refused to attend. The medical personnel used a bullhorn to inform the inmates that medical staff would wait for five minutes at the Alpha Unit door. The inmates ignored the broadcast and the medical staff returned to the jail infirmary. Tension among the inmates continued to escalate. The shift ended and I headed for a workout and chow prior to the deliberate assault rehearsal.

Rehearsals are a vital component of preparing for an assault, and the HRT typically doesn't have the luxury of rehearsing in a replica building of the crisis site. In most instances, the HRT conducts rehearsals by referring to the floor plans of the crisis site for room dimensions and then locating a gymnasium or large field where the crisis site dimensions can be reproduced by using chalk or engineer's tape on the floor and stakes in a field. Operators leave blank spaces to represent doors and windows. The HRT maps out each level of a structure, and every detail—stairs, closets, hallways—is represented.

Once the HRT has reproduced the floor plan for the crisis site, each assault team lines up and methodically goes through its room-clearing movements. Every aspect of available intelligence is included in the rehearsals. The breachers go through the motions of setting the charges. If a hot spot—a known or suspected location of hostages—has been determined, then the movement of the assault team will be directed toward the hot spot with a degree of immediacy to counter any attempts by the hostage takers to harm the hostages. Once the hostages are located and secured, operators set up hostage corridors in which operators post at various locations to direct hostages out of the crisis site. During the rehearsals, other operators role-play as hostages to allow the assault teams the opportunity to escort hostages out of the crisis site. Once everyone has been evacuated from the crisis site, a separate holding area is designated for all hostages, any medical emergencies, any terrorist/hostage takers, and any "unknowns." "Unknowns" may include hostages who have fallen victim to the Stockholm Syndrome or have been identified by other hostages as hostage-taker sympathizers.

At 1700 hours, the HRT mustered and prepared to move to the Bravo Unit. The assault teams were instructed to wear green flight suits and balaclavas. No assault gear would be necessary for the initial walk-through of the Bravo Unit. The HRT moved by foot to the Bravo Unit following a route that traversed behind the medium-security units to prevent the inmates in Alpha Unit from seeing the movement. No need to panic the Cuban inmates into believing an assault was underway.

The HRT regrouped behind Bravo Unit out of view of Alpha Unit. I knew no matter how much we tried to conceal our rehearsals, the communication network among the inmates would get the word to the Cuban inmates that preparation for an assault was underway.

And "trustees" are not the only conduit for passing information; inmates use numerous other means, including jail chaplains, jail nurses, and even the guards who knowingly or unknowingly pass tidbits of information the inmates can piece together. Say one of the law enforcement personnel is standing in line during chow and mentions that rehearsals went well. An inmate who is serving the food will absolutely overhear this tidbit of information and, now, that tidbit is in the communications network, and it will only be a matter of time before it spreads throughout the facility. Operational security (OPSEC) is a must in this environment. We entered the Bravo Unit through a back door.

I immediately recognized the distinct features of a jail: the institutional signs displaying facility rules and the lines on the floor and walls that were not to be crossed by inmates when moving from one point to another. Other features included the overabundance of doors and barred gates separating various holding areas; the high-wattage fluorescent lights that replace the sun, making day and night indistinguishable; and the control room where jail personnel view CCTV monitors, which provide live feedback from surveillance cameras positioned throughout the facility. Also in the control room is the secure metal box containing the internal keys to the facility. From within the control room, jail personnel electronically operate the opening and closing of doors and gates by pushing a menu of buttons displayed on a panel resembling something out of "mission control."

BOP personnel conducted an internal tour of the facility so all of the assault teams would be generally familiar with the room configuration. The BOP personnel explained that the Bravo Unit was not *exactly* configured like the Alpha Unit. Some minor differences existed, but generically speaking both units were the same square footage and similarly organized in terms of number of cells, location of recreation and shower areas, and door placement. In addition, the type of doors, windows, and wall materials were the same in both units, as was the construction. This was vitally important for the breachers in terms of deciding what degree of explosive charges and mechanical breaching equipment would be necessary in the event of an assault.

A BOP employee, normally assigned to FCI Talladega, was attached to each HRT assault team. The BOP employee would join the line of march during an assault and would maintain various keys to the facility. As doors were encountered, the BOP employee would come forward and unlock the door if it was decided the door didn't need to be explosively or mechanically breached. As we moved through the Bravo Unit, I noticed many of the inmates were still locked in their respective cells. The windows in the individual cell doors were covered on the outside with dark paper so the inmates couldn't watch our rehearsals. After becoming familiar with the internal configuration of the Bravo Unit, the assault teams moved back to the front lobby. There, each assault team divided to discuss individual team responsibilities as outlined in the Deliberate Assault Plan. Hotel team was tasked with entering the facility through the "white" side main lobby door.

All crisis site structures are tactically described by the same designations. The front of the structure is referred to as the "white" side, the right side when facing the structure is the "red" side, the left side is the "green" side, and the back of the structure is the "black" side. All windows and doors also receive an alphanumeric designator. For example, when looking at the front or "white side" of a crisis site, the first window or door located to the far left on the ground level is Alpha One. Moving from left to right, the second window or door is Alpha Two and so on. On the second level, the first door or window located to the far left is Bravo One and so on. This alphanumeric and color-coded system for designating sides and openings in a structure allows for consistent nomenclature when the deployed sniper/observers are reporting intel to the command post. It also enables the operations order to be drafted and briefed in a fashion that reduces confusion when discussing tactics associated with the crisis site.

With respect to the Alpha Unit, Hotel team would enter the facility through the "white side" main entrance, designated as Alpha Six. This entry would be made following an explosive breach of the external doors. Upon entry, Hotel team would have the responsibility of clearing the front lobby and adjacent rooms while hastily moving to any known locations of the hostages.

J. D. directed Hotel team to line up in the lobby just inside the front door of the Bravo Unit. We were not going to be able to rehearse our entry because it would be in view of the Alpha Unit. As always, I was designated the point man, first in the line of march. I preferred this assignment. This way there were no distractions. I chose not to be a breacher, an EMT, or any of the other specialty positions that were included in the lineup. I never wanted any other collateral duties. My mission was clear. Enter the crisis site and save the hostages. There would be no deviation from this mission.

When the HRT deployed to FCI Talladega, several former operators, who had recently left the Team and returned to various FBI field divisions as SWAT team leaders, were contacted. These former operators, upon their arrival to FCI Talladega, would be attached to various assault teams. One of the guys, who was an operator before I joined the HRT, was assigned to Hotel. I didn't know anything about the guy, but apparently he was known to be very aggressive and headstrong. Day six began with this guy storming around looking for his missing bottle of shampoo. He barged into the room Dave and I shared and asked if we "borrowed" his shampoo. Dave asked him, "What kind of shampoo is it?" The guy answered, "Prell." I looked at him and said, "I have a bottle of Prell; I found it in the shower. Would you like to borrow some?" The guy just looked at me and didn't know what to say. Then he turned around and left the room. Dave busted out laughing. He said, "Scarhead, no one has ever fronted that guy off before." I turned to Dave and said, "I wasn't fronting the guy off. I offered to loan him some." I grabbed my towel and Prell shampoo and headed toward the showers.

The rehearsals the night before had lasted until around 2200 hours. Hotel team had successfully completed the walk-through of our designated area of responsibility. This evening another rehearsal was scheduled. This one would be a full dress rehearsal. That meant black flight suits and all of the assault gear.

As day shift began, Dave and I took our positions in the emergency assault Suburban. Negotiations had been going on since daybreak. The inmates had already refused another sick call. During the course of conversations with the inmates, one of the Cubans, Jorge Marquez, told negotiators that he was one of five inmates the Cubans had selected to represent them during all future negotiations. Later that afternoon, a forty-one-minute phone call took place between the inmate representatives and the negotiators, during which a sick call was agreed to. During the sick call, the HRT security element noticed that the barred external gate on the front of the Alpha Unit, which led into the breezeway where Hotel team would make entry, was secured shut with a lock and chain. This was critical information. Before an explosive charge could be placed on the front door, the chain would have to be cut with bolt cutters. One more piece of gear the breacher would need to carry forward in the event of an assault. The sick call also raised concerns about the availability of food. The crisis was in day six and, to date, no food had been delivered to the inmates or hostages. In addition, a review of the jail commissary records for the weeks prior to the uprising revealed that each inmate in Alpha Unit had spent less than three dollars per week for food items. This amount of money was not enough to sustain the inmates and the hostages with food.

At 1900 hours, the HRT once again regrouped and moved over to Bravo Unit. Once inside, we would again go through our individual assault team movements. During this rehearsal, we had members of the FBI's regional SWAT teams join us. During a deliberate assault, the SWAT teams would enter the crisis site after the HRT initially secured the hostages. Upon a verbal command, the SWAT teams would enter and assist with clearing the numerous jail cells located on two tiers within the facility.

Another consideration worked out during this rehearsal was the need to identify alternate breach points. If an explosive charge failed to detonate or was insufficient to open the door, leaving one of the assault teams unable to gain entry through their respective primary breach point, an alternate breach point needed to be identified in advance. If the alternate breach point was used, the interior movement of the assault team would change and this movement also needed to be rehearsed. In the event an alternate breach became necessary, the respective team breacher would yell, "Alternate breach!" and the assault team would know to move to the predesignated alternate breach location.

While the rehearsals were underway, a disturbance suddenly occured within the Alpha Unit. BOP personnel staged on the perimeter reported that a growing number of inmates could be seen congregating near the front entrance. The inmates were yelling and pushing against the doors. Immediately, additional BOP personnel were moved forward. The HRT was notified of the disturbance and the rehearsals were discontinued. One of the HRT assault teams headed back to the staging area in order to assume emergency assault responsibilities. An FBI SWAT team contingency had been sitting in during the rehearsals. The rest of the HRT returned to the staging area and jocked up in preparation for an assault. From within the Alpha Unit, several windows were broken out and arrows, constructed from the metal rods found in filing cabinets, were launched toward the BOP perimeter. Within minutes, the disturbance ended and the inmates dispersed. According to BOP officials, the inmates had staged the disturbance to test the government's response.

It was evident the frustration level among the inmates was rising. I wondered how long the on-scene commander would allow the situation to simmer. At what point would a call be made to the attorney general requesting authority for a deliberate assault? Did a hostage have to die or be seriously injured first? Newspaper articles were predicting the uprising would end violently. In addition, various attorneys who represented the Cuban inmates were paraphrased as saying, "No bargaining chips remain for the Cubans or the U.S. government. This could easily lead to a violent conclusion."

`Day seven of the crisis` began without any further disturbance from the inmates. Concerns about the hostages continued to escalate, and the media noted that the standoff was about to enter its second week. Hotel team assumed emergency assault responsibility. The shift progressed without incident. At approximately 1600 hours, five negotiators met face-to-face with the five Cuban inmates who, allegedly, had been selected to represent the 121 Cuban inmates inside Alpha Unit. J.D. suggested that Hotel team remain on emergency assault status until after the face-to-face negotiations concluded. This avoided a shift change between assault teams while the negotiations were ongoing. The negotiations concluded around 1700 hours, and Hotel team handed off the emergency assault responsibilities to Echo team.

Dave and I dropped our assault gear in the staging area and were headed toward the cafeteria when the assault supervisor suddenly entered the staging area and sounded off. "Everyone jock up! The inmates are on the roof of the Alpha Unit. TLs, get your teams ready to go in. Let me know over the radio when each team is up. We're operating on Alpha One, secure. I'll be in the CP." He headed back out the door. "Here we go," I said, looking at Dave. Nodding, he answered, "It's showtime, Scar."

Approximately thirty inmates had congregated on the roof of Alpha Unit. They erected a large cross and hung a banner from it. Made from a bed sheet, the banner read, "Please Media—Justice, Freedom, or Death." The inmates held up another banner that read, "We have not been fed for a week, hostages are dying due to shortage of food." Several sheets were draped over the side of the Alpha Unit which read, "We have been abused long enough," "We want the world to know," and "We love you—please pray." The BOP further intensified its perimeter with additional personnel, and large searchlights were brought in and focused on Alpha Unit. The HRT stood by and waited for the command to assault from the OSC. The inmates reacted further by throwing debris at the BOP personnel holding the perimeter. In response, the BOP officers lobbed non-lethal smoke grenades onto the roof of the Alpha Unit.

The subsequent smoke succeeded in dispersing the inmates, and, by 2100 hours, the last of the inmates climbed back down through the ceiling into Alpha Unit.

The HRT assault supervisor came back into the staging area and called the Team together. "Everyone stand down. The inmates have gone back inside. The negotiators are not sure what prompted this behavior. They're unsure if the face-to-face meeting they had today caused this reaction. My read is the environment inside is becoming increasingly unstable. TLs, be prepared to go at any moment. Remember the ten-day rule." The assault supervisor then headed back to the CP.

The ten-day rule referred to the coincidence that many of the past crises the HRT responded to had lasted ten days. Ten days seemed to be the length of time required for hostage takers to break down and either surrender or do something that initiated an assault. We all knew we were about to begin day eight.

Senator Orrin Hatch speaking with the HRT assault team

Demo at HRT Tire House

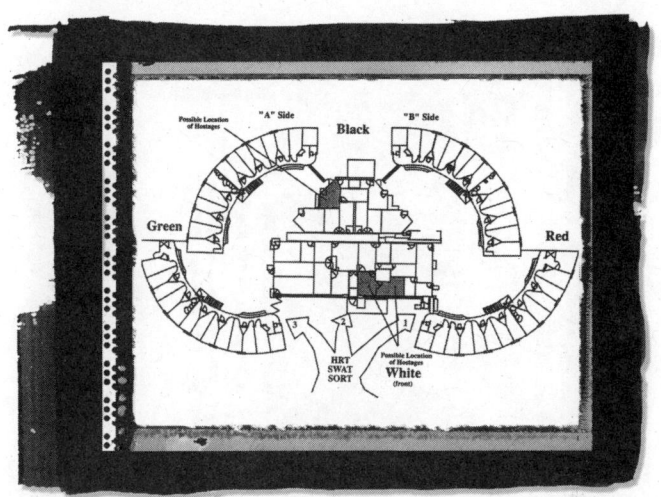

FCI Talladega Alpha Unit floor plan

Hostage release preparations

Forced entry to Alpha Unit

Post assault with HRT team members Dave Corderman (center) and James McGee (right)

Post assault with Hotel team (James McGee 2nd from left and Dave Corderman 2nd from right)

HRT Suburban after breach

HRT Operations Debriefing with Acting U.S. Attorney General William Barr, HRT Commander Dick Rogers, FBI Executive Leadership, and FBI Director William Sessions (from L to R)

FBI Medal of Merit presented to the HRT in recognition of their brave and courageous actions during the Talladega FCI hostage crisis

File No.: Chapter Seven
Subject: Showtime

When the U.S. BOP issued a written press release characterizing the Cuban inmates as "the most difficult, aggressive, violent, and incorrigible inmates ever held in the Bureau of Prisons," Dave and I both agreed this was not a good sign.

Hotel team had the day shift and met at the staging area at 0500 to assume emergency assault responsibilities. It was now day eight, and rehearsals had been preempted the day before by the inmates' stunt on the roof of the Alpha Unit. Rehearsals were back on again at 1700 hours. After donning our gear, J.D. had the team gather around for a quick update. "All right, fellas, you heard the head shed last night. It sounds like things are continuing to deteriorate inside the Alpha Unit. The Cubans are trying to push our buttons. They consider their little demonstration on the roof a victory. Now more than ever we have to stay focused. There are more negotiations planned for today. Word is that a third-party intermediary may be introduced into the negotiation process, so stay alert."

Dave and I headed for the Suburban. After climbing into the front seat I turned to Dave and said, "You know, J.D. is right on target. Inmates are all about manipulation and intimidation. That's how they survive day to day, and fucking with our minds brings them nothing but satisfaction."

"I know Scarhead, but if they keep it up, we're going to fuck with them by shoving an MP5 barrel down their throats."

"It'd better happen soon, or saving the hostages may not be an option."

Like the BOP press release, the introduction of a third-party intermediary was not a good sign. It was a pretty reliable indicator that the negotiation process was running out of options. Exacerbating the situation were media accounts that likened the crisis to an uprising staged by death row inmates who have nothing to lose. A member of the Coalition to Support Cuban Detainees was quoted as saying, "…they want to fight for their freedom. Some would die for their own freedom and they see themselves doing that."

As Dave and I sat in the Suburban, it was suddenly reported that two inmates had again gained access to the roof of the Alpha Unit. They were in the process of hanging two more banners. One read, "We are not hungry for food but for freedom." The other listed three people the Cuban inmates wanted to talk to: Cynthia Corzo, a reporter for *El Nuevo Herald*; Brian Cabell, a CNN correspondent; and Huber Matos Sr., a Miami-based leader in Cuban-American affairs. After erecting the banners without interference, the two inmates climbed back down into the Alpha Unit.

At 1000 hours, it was passed to Hotel team that a third-party intermediary would, in fact, move forward soon. Accompanied by escorts, the intermediary, identified as the Miami-based reporter Cynthia Corzo, would try to make contact with the inmates. Through negotiations, the inmates had tentatively agreed to release a hostage if they could meet face-to-face with Cynthia Corzo. A civilian secretary named Kitty B. Suddeth, who worked for the BOP within the Alpha Unit, was one of the female hostages. Through previous negotiations and the occasional sick call, it was determined that she was in need of medical attention. The goal was to secure her release, but the negotiators were doubtful the inmates would keep their end of the deal.

At 1050 hours, Cynthia Corzo was escorted to the front of the Alpha Unit and given a bullhorn to attempt communication with the Cuban inmates. When Ms. Corzo went forward, Hotel team moved into an escalated state of readiness just in case an emergency assault became necessary. Ms. Corzo raised the bullhorn and pointed it toward the front of the Alpha Unit. She then announced her name and told the inmates this was their opportunity to tell their story. Ms. Corzo informed the inmates that before she could talk to them, Kitty Suddeth needed to be released. There was no response from the inmates. Cynthia Corzo asked a second time for the release of Kitty Suddeth. The inmates refused to comply, and Ms. Corzo was escorted away. Hotel team relinquished emergency assault team duties to Golf team. The scheduled rehearsal in Bravo Unit was pushed back to 2200 hours because of ongoing negotiations regarding the release of Kitty Suddeth.

At 1740 hours, Cynthia Corzo was again escorted to the front of Alpha Unit at the request of the inmates and with the encouragement of the negotiators. Once again, using the bullhorn, she let the inmates know that they needed to release Kitty Suddeth before she could talk to them directly. As Golf team stood by prepared to conduct an emergency assault, the inmates again refused to consummate the release. Ms. Corzo was escorted away from the housing unit a second time. The inmates' indecisiveness was blatant and even expected. I don't think anyone truly trusted that the inmates were good for their word. We're talking hardened criminals who love nothing better than to jerk the chain of law enforcement. Their failure to follow through with the release of one hostage also seemed indicative of a power struggle inside the Alpha Unit among the Cuban inmates.

Within an hour, the inmates again requested that Ms. Corzo be brought forward. Once again, Golf team moved into an enhanced state of readiness and Cynthia Corzo was escorted forward to the Alpha Unit. This time, the inmates brought Kitty Suddeth forward. She was dressed in a blue inmate jumpsuit and looked frail. She was a small, slender woman in her late twenties with light brown, shoulder-length, straight hair. As the inmates released Kitty Suddeth and she passed through the Alpha Unit door to freedom, medical personnel rushed forward to meet her. She began to cry and was physically shaking, but she refused to lie down on a stretcher and walked out of her own accord. Her only comment was, "I'm fine." Kitty Suddeth was immediately transported to the jail infirmary for medical care and an evaluation. She was also reunited with her family at this time. Based upon her medical condition, FBI special agents would, at some point, interview her about the condition of the other hostages, the demeanor of the Cuban inmates, which inmates were in control, the type of weapons the inmates had in their possession, and any other relevant intelligence that could be factored into the negotiation process or a tactical assault.

Within twenty minutes of the release of Kitty Suddeth, the inmates were granted an interview with Cynthia Corzo and her photographer Carlos Guerrero. The interview was conducted in a room, inside Alpha Unit, where bars separated the reporter and cameraman from the inmates. HRT operators provided security for the meeting. Metal folding chairs were provided for everyone to sit on. Details from the meeting were passed to the rest of the HRT during our preshift briefs.

The only inmates present were the five Cuban representatives. Leadership of the group was split between two of the inmates identified as Jorge Marquez Medina and Jesus de Armas. As the inmates arrived for the meeting, they brought another female hostage into the room. Her name was Linda Calhoun, and she was one of the three INS employees taken hostage during the uprising. Ms. Calhoun was allowed to speak to the reporter. In a soft voice, she advised that all of the hostages had been without food for eight days and only water had been provided. She then stated, in front of the five Cuban inmates, that the hostages were not being mistreated. The main problem was hunger. As much as they would have relished the opportunity to snatch and rescue Linda Calhoun, the HRT operators were there to provide security, not attempt to rescue a hostage. Ms. Calhoun stood up from her seat and moved away, surrendering any notion that she would possibly be set free.

Medina stated that the goal of the uprising was to abolish deportation of inmates to Cuba. He stated precisely, "I'm not talking about a moratorium, not a temporary suspension, but that they make it a legal change." The five inmates collectively demanded the formation of a special commission to supervise the status of inmates from the 1980 Mariel boatlift. The inmates further demanded that the commission include anti-Castro activist Huber Matos, United Nations High Commissioner for Refugees Fernando Chang-Muy, U.S. Congressional Representative John Lewis (D-GA), U.S. District Judge Marvin Shoob, Atlanta attorney Gary Leshaw, civil rights activist Coretta Scott King, CNN reporter Brian Cabell, and Cynthia Corzo.

As the meeting between the Cuban inmates and Cynthia Corzo came to an end, Medina stated that along with the remaining nine hostages were eighteen American inmates whom the Cubans also considered hostages. These inmates had been transferred from other units within FCI Talladega to Alpha Unit (more commonly called the Hole) for disciplinary segregation. Medina produced a note from one of the inmate hostages that read, "I am a U.S. prisoner. We are alive. They are treating us well. Please don't do anything to put our lives in danger." The negotiators already knew about the presence of the American inmates within the Alpha Unit. The authenticity of this note was not questioned. It was anticipated, given information derived through overhears, that the Cuban inmates might try to include the American inmates as an additional item to broker with.

The HRT prepared to move to the Bravo Unit for another deliberate assault rehearsal. Repetition was key in ensuring that we conducted tactical movement inside the Alpha Unit dynamically and that we reached the hostages expeditiously. During each rehearsal, we refined our tactics. I memorized the exact number of paces it took for me to "run my route." I knew the exact number of steps I needed to take before turning into an adjoining room after the initial entry, and I knew how many steps it took to reach the back wall of the room. If I needed to, I could run my route blindfolded. The rehearsals also assisted in keeping some of the perishable skills, which are part and parcel of being a CT operator, honed to a razor sharp edge. Not only does CQB require that we practice our own tactical movements, but every operator on the assault team must also understand each position in the line of march. During the assault, an injured operator could change our line of march responsibilities instantaneously.

The ability to fire a weapon is a perishable skill and we had not been able to live fire our weapons for eight days. Instead, we continually dry fired our handguns and our MP5 submachine guns to keep our shooting skills temporarily up to standard. If the crisis extended beyond ten days, however, we would need to get to a shooting range to maintain the surgical shooting skills required for CT operators.

My responsibilities, in the event of a deliberate assault, would commence upon Hotel team mustering at the staging area designated as phase line yellow, the last point of cover and concealment. The team would climb into one of the dark blue Suburbans and drive across the lawn in front of the Alpha Unit where the BOP perimeter was located. Five operators would ride inside the vehicle and four would stand on the running boards attached to the sides of the vehicle exterior. As the driver of the Suburban, I would pull up and stop perpendicular to the Alpha Unit, with the front bumper of the vehicle resting against the exterior brick wall. The vehicle's position would be approximately twenty feet to the left of the main entrance to Alpha Unit. This door had the alphanumeric designator Alpha Six and it was Hotel team's primary breach point. Our alternate breach point was Alpha Four, the door located approximately twenty feet to the left of the Suburban's location. I would place the vehicle in park and turn off the engine.

Once the vehicle came to rest against the wall, all of the Hotel team operators would dismount from the vehicle and line up against the wall in their predesignated order. Included in Hotel team's line of march was one BOP employee who maintained the keys that we might need to open some of the doors encountered on the inside of the Alpha Unit. Each operator would hunker down in a line parallel to and against the exterior wall of the Alpha Unit between where the Suburban was parked and Alpha Six.

I would exit the Suburban through the driver's door, move toward the rear, and open the back cargo doors. I would then grab a body-length ballistic blast shield. The Hotel team breacher would grab the preconstructed explosive breaching charge. We would then both move toward the wall and get in position. Once in position, I would be number one in the line of march—the point man. As of this moment, my concentration would be on covering our movement forward. I would switch my MP5 selector off safe, and I would engage and eliminate any threat appearing to our front. I would position the blast shield in front of me to help deflect any flying debris, shrapnel, and the over-pressure from the charge I would encounter in my position as number one.

The team breacher, and the number two man as cover, would then move forward to place the charge. The Alpha Six door was located inside an alcove, which was a ninety-degree turn to the left from where I was positioned. To reach the door, we would have to open another barred door, which was secured by a chain and padlock. This was the chain and lock the security detail had first observed during one of the sick calls. As the number two man provided cover down the alcove, the breacher would cut the chain with bolt cutters and then swing the barred door open. The breacher would follow the number two man, who now had the point, down the alcove to the Alpha Six door. Once they reached the door, the breacher would affix the explosive charge, and attach and unroll the shock tube. The shock tube provides the necessary distance between the charge and where the operators are staged. If a safe distance is not achieved, the over-pressure from the charge coupled with flying debris can be deadly. With the number two man continuing to provide cover on the Alpha Six door, they would both move back toward the location of the rest of Hotel team, stringing the shock tube along the ground as they moved. As they passed my position, I would resume the point, and the number two man would fall back into the line of march behind me. The breacher would fall back into his predesignated position as number four and attach the shock tube to the shooter, which, when fired, would detonate the explosive breaching charge.

Once the breacher was satisfied that the charge was ready, he would give J.D. the thumbs-up. The number two man would look over my shoulder to confirm that I had the selector switch on my MP5 off safe. He would then give a thumbs-up with his left hand and each operator would repeat the signal to the operator to their rear indicating they were ready. Once the last man in the line of march received this signal, he would give the man in front of him a "squeeze-back" to confirm he was ready. The squeeze-back would be repeated until it reached me.

J.D. would then contact the HRT commander, Alpha One, via his radio and advise that Hotel team was at phase line green—the breach point, the point of no return. Alpha One would confirm Hotel team was ready and then we would all wait until the other assault teams advised that they were at phase line green. Once all of the teams were in position, Alpha One would commence the countdown, beginning at five. When he reached one, the breaching charges would be detonated. The sound of the blast would be the signal to initiate the assault.

Once the assault was initiated, I would move forward and turn ninety degrees into the alcove facing the Alpha Six door, continuing to engage any threat I encountered. I would then move toward the Alpha Six door. I knew the door was nine unobstructed paces after I made the turn. Once through the door, I would enter the lobby and turn ninety degrees to the left, continuing to engage any threat. My first responsibility was to move along the left lobby wall and enter and clear the first room I came to on my left. According to the floor plans and the room configuration within Bravo Unit, this room was eight paces deep. After clearing this room and verbally announcing to the rest of Hotel team that the room was clear, I would then verbally announce I was "coming out" and reenter the lobby. Once back in the lobby, I would continue my route to the left and enter the next room I came to. This room was larger than the first room and was eleven paces deep. After clearing this room, I would follow the same procedures as before, reenter the lobby and then move along the lobby wall until I reached the doorway leading into the hallway adjacent to the rear of the lobby. Once there, I would enter the hallway, move ninety degrees to the left, and stage there until further advised.

During a deliberate assault, the HRT operates pursuant to the FBI's deadly force policy. In a nutshell, this policy states that FBI agents can employ deadly force when they are confronted with an adversary whose actions lead the special agent to believe his life or the life of another is threatened or in danger of grave physical harm. On its face, the deadly force policy is relatively clear as to when deadly force can be applied. However, within the world of counterterrorism and hostage rescue, further understanding of the rules of engagement is required. Upon entry into the crisis site behind the explosive breach, it is understood that the hostage takers know the gig is up. In other words, an assault is underway and the hostage takers will be making their way to the hostages with the implied intent to do the hostages harm. Between the time of entry and the moment the hostages are located and secured, the operators are prepared to kill anyone who fails to comply with their demands to get down and/or impedes their movement to the location of the hostages. If an unarmed inmate rushes at me during the initial stages of the assault and does not comply with my commands, he will be shot. This is necessary because the inmate may be trying to delay my movement to the hostages in order to give other inmates time to harm the hostages.

Once the hostages have been located and secured, the need to apply deadly force is less likely. The assault continues, but the movement of the assaulter slows down. The necessity to reach and save the hostages no longer exists. The mission evolves into a law enforcement clear, which requires that the entire crisis site be searched and declared safe. During this stage, if an unarmed inmate rushes an operator, the inmate is ordered to get down; if the inmate fails to comply, then methods other than deadly force are applied. This can include using a stun gun, which fires an electric shock, using a collapsible baton, firing rubber bullets, employing tear gas, or using physical confrontation in the form of control holds, which, when applied effectively, take the inmate to the floor and achieve submission. As HRT operators, we each carried a collapsible baton and pepper spray, which we could use to achieve compliance in the event verbal commands didn't work. Deadly force can still be applied if the operator determines the situation requires such an action.

In any situation in which a special agent chooses to use deadly force, his decision will ultimately be examined and scrutinized ad nauseam. A career in law enforcement is best defined as twenty years of mundane paperwork and routine boredom interrupted by rare seconds of bloodcurdling terror and danger when the law enforcement officer must make split-second decisions that will be second-guessed for decades. When a special agent uses deadly force, he must be able to precisely describe the situation that required such an action and he must articulate the recollection with flawless accuracy every time he is asked. This requirement to recall the facts can extend for decades.

The ability to function effectively in a law enforcement environment that is subject to such a high degree of scrutiny is the essence of an HRT operator. This capability is what the HRT selection process seeks to reveal and confirm in those special agents who possess the courage and desire to try out. Most don't make the cut. Unlike the military where terms like "acceptable losses, collateral damage, and suppressive fire" are included in the operations order, an HRT operator must account for every round fired, and the margin of error is zero.

The rehearsal that night ended around midnight. The HRT moved back to the staging area, and each team, except for the one scheduled for the night shift, prepared to hit the rack. Some of the operators took some time to dry fire and then wipe down their weapons. Dave and I made sure our respective gear was in order and then turned out the lights.

Day nine came early, and as I rolled out of bed I looked over at Dave and said, "Three hots and a cot." Dave was just waking up and replied, "Yeah, Scarhead, this is like being at a Club Med resort." We both got up and started the morning routine all over again. This was a day off from emergency assault duty for Hotel team, and we could use the break for gear prep.

After a breakfast of French toast, Hotel team mustered in the same corner of the staging area where our gear was stored. J.D. passed around a number of photographs. "Take a look at these photos. These are the Cuban inmates who have been identified so far as the ringleaders on the inside. The first photo in the package is Jorge Marquez Medina. The second photo is Jesus de Armas. These seem to be the primary leaders. Based upon overhears and information derived from the hostage who was recently released, there is a power struggle going on inside the Alpha Unit between these two Cubans. The rest of the photos are of other Cuban inmates who have been observed by the snipers or were identified by the released hostages as possibly being involved in any decisions the inmates collectively make."

I looked at the photos. These inmates were no different from the numerous dirt bags I had dealt with in the Ventura County jails. I reflected back on an Interview and Interrogation class I had taken as a new agent in the Academy. The instructor had explained to the class, "…when interviewing a potential subject, never position yourself so the subject has to look up at you. This may offend him and make him feel like you're talking down to him. You must be sensitive to his cultural norms. You can't offend his machismo." What a crock of crap. Later during the class, the instructor had asked me to come forward and attempt to interview him. He would pose as a potential subject who was already in custody. I moved to the front of the class. I told the instructor to sit down and then I stood over him and began my interview. He immediately "took offense" and started to develop an attitude. I told him the same thing I told numerous inmates when I was a Deputy Sheriff, "You don't have to talk to me. The entire jail population knows you're in here being interviewed, and when I walk out of here, if you continue with the attitude, I'm going to let it be overheard that you took the cheese, you ratted out everyone. Guess what will happen to you next?" The class instructor stopped the interview. Apparently, he had never been confronted with this technique.

As I continued to scan the photos, I remembered the intelligence BOLO (Be On the Look Out) that had come to the Ventura County jail in the early '80s describing the tattoos and scarring indicative of Mariel boatlift Cubans who might be entering the jail population. One of the key identifiers was a tattoo located on the inside of the bottom lip. This was how Castro had marked his career criminals before he released them and sent them to America.

J.D. continued, "Once you've all taken a look at the photos, pass them back to me. They're available in the CP along with an NCIC printout for each of these scumbags." Just like the National Crime Information Center (NCIC) printout I had used when I arrested Gregory Dewey Clifford back in Albuquerque, the Cuban inmates each had a criminal history on record in the system. Photos like these were typically pinned to a bulletin board inside the CP along with photos of the hostages. In addition, other pertinent information, like emergency phone numbers and scheduled meetings were either printed and posted, or written on butcher paper and taped to the walls of the CP.

J.D. passed on more information, which FBI investigators had retrieved during their interviews of the released hostages. "Last night the inmates and the hostages were fed. Based on information we got directly from the recently released female hostage and from her medical examination, it looks like the hostages have had little to no food or water since this crisis began. The inmates are making a big deal about it, as if we're to blame, but the negotiators confirmed that there has been no mention of food during their conversations with the inmates. This is just another orchestrated effort by the inmates to sway the media. Nevertheless, they all got fed just past midnight. The meal included ground beef, beans, rice, and bread. The female hostage also reported that one of the hostages is ill. Possibly a mild heart attack. This hasn't been confirmed."

I looked over at Dave. We were both thinking the same thing. We might *actually* conduct an assault. Things were deteriorating to the point that someone was going to have to step up to the plate and make a decision. Deliberate assault would not be a popular choice. The last time law enforcement authorities assaulted a jail was at Attica Correctional Facility[18] in New York some twenty years earlier. That assault resulted in a blood bath that left twenty-nine inmates and ten hostages dead.

"Listen guys," J.D. continued, "if we do go through with an assault, the initial explosive charge is going to sound like the beginning of World War III. The entry charges have been built and prototypes have been tested. The breachers can confirm this, but it looks like we're good to go." J.D. was correct. The master breacher for the HRT along with several of the individual assault team breachers had traveled to another federal penitentiary and actually tested the charges by blowing doors at that facility. This was a first. This test enabled the breachers to calculate the exact weight of the explosives needed to get us through the entry door. Jails provide a unique target because they're designed to keep inmates locked inside and everyone else outside.

J.D. finished the meeting by stating, "Listen guys, stay alert today. Get your gear squared away and then stay in the area. When you go to PT, keep checking in. Things could go to shit in a heartbeat."

I turned to Dave and said, "Let's wipe down the weapons. Make sure they're good to go and then get in a grinder." Dave agreed. An hour in the Federal Prison Industries warehouse knocking out a run coupled with push-ups, pull-ups, and sit-ups would get the blood flowing.

After the workout, we headed toward the chow hall. As we walked past the BOP perimeter, I noticed the SORT guys were in the process of firing up several barbecue pits. The wind was blowing directly toward the Alpha Unit and the smoke was blowing in that direction. Soon the smell of steaks on the grill would engulf the entire Alpha Unit. Both Dave and I agreed that this should instigate a reaction from the inmates, and we were both correct.

A little past noon, five Cuban inmates again emerged from the Alpha Unit with banners in hand to hang on the roof. This was the third day in a row inmates had climbed out onto the roof of the facility. Dave and I hustled back to where our gear was staged and stood by. The inmates stayed on the roof for about thirty minutes and hung two more banners. One stated, "Pray for us." The other read, "Warden, don't lie anymore." The inmates also fastened a large Cuban flag to a pole so it could fly over the building. All five inmates then climbed back down into the Alpha Unit.

That afternoon, the negotiators were again able to convince the inmates to have a face-to-face meeting. The meeting was scheduled for 1615 hours and would once again include the inmate negotiation committee of five Cubans. During the meeting, the Cubans agreed to a sick call later that evening if more food would in turn be delivered. The Cubans then issued a caveat. They had collected each hostage's jail identification card and placed it into a pillowcase. If more food was not delivered, they would select a name from the pillowcase and that hostage would be killed. They would either throw the hostage from the roof of the facility or stab the hostage to death. If for any reason the inmates determined a hostage needed to die, this type of lottery system would be the mechanism for selecting the victim. The meeting ended at 1715 hours.

Immediately following the meeting, a sick call was arranged. The medical personnel along with the security detail walked toward the front of Alpha Unit pushing a cart filled with various medical supplies and medicine. As the hostages were brought forward for a visual examination to determine their physical condition and well-being, one of the female hostages waved and made a motion with her hand that alarmed the medical personnel. It seemed she was attempting to wave good-bye. It also seemed she was trying to send a message indicating the hostages were in danger of physical harm. Each of the hostages displayed a solemn demeanor as the sick call progressed. As the sick call ended, there was an atmosphere of impending danger. The medical personnel, escorted by the security personnel, headed back to the CP to report their observations to the on-scene commander (OSC).

At 1900 hours, the HRT was summoned to muster in the area designated as a briefing room, adjacent to where our assault gear was staged. We all grabbed metal chairs and sat down. Then ASAC Dick

Rogers, commander of the HRT, and another gentleman walked into the room. Commander Rogers was wearing his black Nomex flight suit. His movement was rigid and he looked worn from lack of sleep. His expression was one of resolute decisiveness regarding what he was about to say. "Gentlemen, the lives of the nine hostages who remain inside the Alpha Unit are in serious danger. The situation has deteriorated to the point that Director Sessions has decided a deliberate assault is required to save the hostages' lives. This is the type of mission you men train for. I am certain we will succeed."

ASAC Rogers then turned toward the man who had entered the room with him. He introduced him as the SAC of the Birmingham Division of the FBI. FCI Talladega fell within the immediate jurisdiction of the Birmingham Field Office. ASAC Rogers said, "Men, the SAC would like to say a few words."

This guy appeared to be between forty-five and fifty years old. He was dressed in the stereotypical dark suit common to FBI management. He looked out across the fifty HRT operators who were waiting to hear his comments before they got busy with the task at hand of saving the lives of the hostages. "All right, I noticed when I was walking over here from the CP that there are a lot of cigarette butts lying in the grass outside. I want to make it clear that leaving cigarette butts lying around will not be tolerated. I want that area policed up."

I couldn't believe my ears. If this moron said anything else, no one heard it. Who did this dumbass think he was talking to? Apparently, this goof didn't realize that no one on the HRT smokes. It's an unwritten rule that smokers don't make it through the selection process. Once again, the Peter Principle rang true. Managers rise to their highest level of incompetence. This mope couldn't carry the jockstrap of the operators he was addressing. We were about to put our lives on the line to save nine hostages, and the mission would be successful in spite of this dipshit and the other ego-driven, self-consumed micromanagers who permeated the ranks of the FBI.

The HRT commander and the SAC left the room and the assault supervisor took the floor. Now it *was* showtime.

File No.: Chapter Eight
Subject: French Toast for Breakfast

Three hundred Spartan warriors of ancient Hellas donned their armored breastplates and Corinthian helmets. They maneuvered their bronze shields and honed swords into position for battle. They waited patiently, as they had hundreds of times before, in preparation for this moment. What it took to be a Spartan warrior—the grueling rites of passage, the relentless training regimen, and the disciplined warrior-lifestyle—required sacrifice, but created self-confidence and a quiet resolve. Indeed, this sacrifice would pay dividends as they prepared to defend all of Greece at the narrow pass of Thermopylae.

The HRT assault supervisor moved to the front of the briefing room. He was wearing his black Nomex flight suit. His 9mm Browning Hi-Power pistol was holstered and hanging from his assault rig around his waist. The room grew quiet, deathly quiet, as he surveyed the operators with his "thousand-yard stare." This look is a product of intensity and focus. It is not a natural expression. It develops through years of intense training and a willingness to push the envelope. It is a look that testifies to being in the line of fire, accepting the challenge, and conquering adversity. It is symbolic of the ancient warrior lifestyle.

"TLs and operators give me your undivided attention. This is the operations order for tomorrow's mission. Tomorrow morning at 0330 hours, the HRT supported by regional FBI SWAT teams and

Federal Bureau of Prison SORTs will conduct a deliberate assault on Federal Correctional Institution Talladega, Alabama. This assault is necessary in order to rescue nine hostages being held by 121 Cuban inmates housed in the maximum security Alpha Unit within this facility. Intelligence indicates leadership among the Cuban inmates is divided and the hostages are in imminent danger of being harmed or killed." The assault supervisor began the process of issuing a five-paragraph operations order to the assault element and its supporting entities. The five paragraphs, abbreviated as SMEAC, would include the subheadings Situation, Mission, Execution, Administrative/Logistics, and Command/Control.

"Let me elaborate some on the situation. The attorney general considers this uprising an act of terrorism.[19] Therefore, our mission is clear. We will assault the Alpha Unit, locate and secure the hostages, and eliminate with extreme prejudice anyone who attempts to obstruct our movement to rescue the hostages. With that said, keep in mind, as always, we operate pursuant to the FBI's deadly force policy." By the FBI's definition, an act of terrorism is a criminal act conducted in furtherance of a political agenda. The Cuban inmates were, by admission, attempting to fulfill their articulated political agenda, and there was no doubt the uprising and subsequent taking of hostages was intended to create terror.

The assault supervisor continued with the execution phase of the OPORD. "We will muster here tomorrow morning at 0300 hours. Execution of the assault will be in accordance with the rehearsals we've been conducting at Bravo Unit. I am not going to go into explicit details regarding the tactics associated with the assault. I expect each TL to verbally go over these details with his respective team. I encourage each assaulter to then provide a brief-back so there is no confusion about individual movement and responsibilities. The environment will be dark and confusing. I don't want a cross-fire situation to develop."

The brief-back is a common SOP, and it accomplishes exactly what the assault supervisor wanted. It requires each operator to verbally repeat his individual duties and reconfirms the stated mission through repetition. This helps to reduce confusion and forces each operator to articulate his individual responsibilities during the assault. Conducting a brief-back helps to reduce the concern for cross-fire situations. This is especially true in situations requiring multiple entry points by the assault teams. In this instance, the HRT would be entering through three breach points if everything went as planned. At some point during the assault, the teams would eventually link up. Ongoing communication and staying alert to your surroundings were fundamental in terms of preventing a deadly cross fire. In addition to brief-backs, the HRT routinely trains at a level that further minimizes the chance of cross fire. Target identification as well as keying on the threat assist in reducing the chance of operators becoming confused and shooting at each other. Fire discipline, communication, sound tactics, and strict adherence to running your designated route will prevent a cross-fire situation from developing. CQB is not the place for individuals intent on thinking outside the box.

"After we muster here in the morning, I will provide any last minute developments, specifically any further intelligence on the location of hot spots. Once each assault team is positioned in its respective assault vehicle, the TL will notify the HRT commander. This position is designated as phase line yellow. Once everyone is in place and ready, you will be directed to move to phase line green with compromise authority. Once the breaching charges have been placed and the TLs have advised the HRT commander that their respective team is ready, the countdown will commence. The breaching charges will be fired on one, the assault will occur on the Execute command. The entry points are currently identified as White Side Alpha Four, Alpha Six, and Alpha Eight. Each assault team is aware of its primary and alternate breach points."

Compromise authority allows any operator to verbally sound off if he thinks the hostage takers have compromised the assault team movement to phase line green. In this case, the HRT commander must decide whether to initiate the assault immediately to save the hostages. If all hostages are not together, there may be more than one hot spot. Being in possession of intelligence that identifies the possible location of the hot spot(s) allows the assault teams to adjust their tactics and move directly to the location of the hostages.

"FBI regional SWAT will stage at phase line yellow and await the direction to move forward. Once the hostages have been secured and evacuated, regional SWAT will be directed to move forward and coordinate with the HRT assault elements before making entry. Upon entry, the regional SWAT teams will assist with clearing any remaining areas within the Alpha Unit. Regional SWAT will also assist with securing, controlling, cuffing, searching, and ultimately turning over to BOP SORT all inmates inside the Alpha Unit. The BOP SORT perimeter will remain intact during the assault. Each assault team will have their predesignated BOP attachment with them during the assault to assist with opening doors inside the Alpha Unit. Be advised, the snipers reported that the inmates have fortified the roof access they've been climbing through during the past few days. Sniper/observer teams will remain in place during the assault to ensure inmates do not regain access to the roof in an attempt to escape or engage law enforcement authorities from above."

The assault supervisor then moved into the administrative phase of the OPORD, the segment where FBI executive management grants authorizations and policies are reiterated. "As I mentioned earlier, we will be operating in accordance with the FBI deadly force policy. It is unclear which weapons the inmates may have in their possession. To date, they have been seen with homemade knives, spears, bows and arrows, and clubs."

I was concerned about what weapons the inmates might possess. I knew from my experience working in jails that inmates can be very creative. In addition to the weapons we knew about, they had easy access to various cleaning and medical supplies. Containers of detergent could be poured onto the tile floors to create a slippery surface to slow down any assault. Bleach and other caustic chemicals could be thrown in the eyes of law enforcement. The inmates had access to syringes and antiseptics. Any of the flammable liquids could easily be fashioned into Molotov cocktails, which could be thrown at law enforcement and ignite a fire. Surgical tubing could be fashioned into slingshots, which could launch a half-inch hex nut at a deadly velocity. Other booby traps included trip wires and lightbulbs filled with a flammable liquid that makes them explode when the wall switch is turned on.

The inmates also had access to some of the riot gear left by BOP personnel, including Mace and pepper spray. I also knew they could manufacture crude firearms. The "zip gun" is a weapon first confiscated at Folsom State Prison in California. Several members of the notorious Mexican Mafia (La eMe)[20] were sentenced to Folsom. To continue to carry out their gangland hits, members of La eMe developed the zip gun. The weapon is constructed from paper magazines fashioned into hard papier-mâché and rolled to form a rigid barrel. Plastic bottle caps are melted to seal the end of the barrel, ground match heads are used as an ignition source, and sharpened pencil leads serve as a projectile. The match heads are ground up and the powder is poured into the sealed end of the barrel. A fuse is left protruding from this end. The projectile is then dropped into the open end of the barrel. When the fuse is lit, the match-head powder ignites. The gases from the ignition expand and fire the projectile out the end of the barrel. A zip gun is capable of firing one lethal round at close range that can penetrate half-inch plywood.

"The SAC has approved the use of flash-bangs," the assault supervisor continued. The initial entry would not require deployment of a flash-bang because an explosive breach would be used. The HRT is the only tactical team within the FBI authorized to use explosives for breaching purposes. The explosive breach would provide two services. First, it would blow the door, thus providing entry to the assault teams. Second, it would do the job of a flash-bang by creating a diversion that would temporarily distract the inmates. Standard FBI policy requires the SAC to approve the utilization of flash-bangs. It must be articulated to the SAC that the deployment of flash-bangs is a necessary diversion to accomplish the mission. After the initial explosive breach, we would use flash-bangs to gain access into subsequent rooms.

"Medical personnel are on standby in the event of an injury. We will evacuate medical emergencies in the following order: hostages first, followed by law enforcement, then inmates and terrorists. Everyone is to remember the Alpha Unit is a crime scene. FBI Evidence Response Teams will process the facility once the hostages are rescued. FBI SWAT and BOP SORT will secure the facility. Be cognizant of potential evidence and any spontaneous statements made by the inmates. TLs, keep in mind that in the event a weapon is discharged, a shooting review will follow."

As always, HRT operators would be performing a hostage rescue, but their responsibilities did not end there. They were also expected to function as FBI special agents and be prepared to testify in a court of law if necessary. This is one of the most prominent distinctions between HRT operators and the rest of the world's CT community operators.

The assault supervisor then prepared to deliver the final paragraph of the OPORD. This would address communications as well as command and control issues. "We will be operating on Alpha One-Secure as the assault net. The snipers will initially be on Alpha Two-Secure. The snipers will 'jacket rabbit' from the sniper net to the assault net when all elements are at phase line yellow and directed to move to phase line green. ASAC Dick Rogers is the tactical commander during this operation. He will give the command to execute, and he will decide if at any time there is a need to abort the mission. The inmates have threatened to kill a hostage if they are not fed. Tonight a meal will be delivered to the inmates. Included with the meal will be an abundance of decaffeinated coffee. It is anticipated that the inmates will eat well and then fall asleep. We will reconvene at 0300 hours. Let's conduct a time hack. My watch has 2045 hours. TLs set your watches to mine. I'll see everyone in the morning."

As Dave and I headed back to the staging area to ensure our assault gear was ready to go, we agreed that feeding the inmates prior to the assault was an ingenious idea. They were sure to gorge themselves and then fall asleep. Early morning has historically been the best time to initiate an assault. I had worked enough graveyard shifts to know that the toughest time to stay awake was between 0300 and 0500. During the sleep cycle, these are the hours when most people are in deep sleep, and the most vulnerable.

I made it into the rack by 2230 hours after providing J.D. with a concise brief-back and inventorying my assault gear half a dozen times. Then, with the help of several other operators, I rigged the Hotel and Echo team Suburbans with assault ladders.

Two single-wide assault ladders were aligned parallel to one another and attached to the front rail of the aluminum platforms that rest on top of each Suburban. The ladders were attached to a swivel so they could be raised and then leaned against the side of the Alpha Unit. This would give us access to the roof of the structure if it became necessary.

As I lay down, I was confident that within several hours nine hostages would be rescued. I reflected back to when I had decided to join the HRT. The same thought went through my mind: *Failure is not an option.*

`I slept soundly until 0200` and then awoke at the exact time I'd set my mental alarm clock. I stood up and slowly conducted a final inspection of my assault gear. With the exception of the American flag attached to the upper sleeve of my right arm with Velcro, I was dressed in black, including my Nomex flight suit, balaclava, gloves, as well as my socks, elbow and kneepads, and Adidas GSG9 assault boots. I had on my black Level II ballistic helmet in lieu of the favored, lightweight, non-ballistic Pro-Tec helmet I normally wore. Covering the head with some ballistic protection was a good idea given the potential for flying shrapnel from the exposure to the explosive door charge. My clear lens Bolle goggles were in place and hadn't fogged up yet even in the humid conditions of Alabama during August. More than once, I'd been in situations where the goggles had fogged up and the only remedy was to remove them. Nowadays the goggles have a little blower fan that keeps them clear. I repositioned the radio earpiece in my left ear. There was no radio traffic at the moment. Noise discipline was being exercised.

The body armor carrier I had on weighed approximately fifty

pounds and included Level IIIA ballistic inserts, which overlapped under the arms to provide protection from most handgun rounds. A ceramic ballistic plate, designed to stop rifled rounds, was inserted into a pocket sewn on the front of the carrier. This provided me with ballistic protection directly over the center of mass where most of my vital organs are located. A small pillow was placed between the ceramic plate and my chest to help absorb the blunt trauma associated with the energy generated from a striking round.

Inside the pockets on the front of the carrier was a Mini Maglite and a collapsible ASP baton. The Maglite had red lens capability for low-light illumination to reduce the chance of compromise. The ASP baton could be used to break a window or deliver a less-than-lethal blow to an inmate who failed to comply.

Inside the pecker pad hanging from the front of my body armor, was a notebook and pen, some extra flex-cuffs and a couple of extra thirteen-round magazines loaded with 9mm Hydra-Shok ammunition for the two Browning Hi-Power auto-loader pistols. The pistol equipped with a SureFire flashlight was in my assault holster. The other was my backup and was located in a holster attached to the body armor carrier over my chest. The Hydra-Shok ammunition delivers a devastating blow to the target. As a subsonic round, it achieves suitable penetration, but does not pass completely through the human body. The tip of the round is a hollow point. This allows the round to spread out on impact and deliver maximum damage to the internal organs. Both handguns were single action, locked and loaded with tritium night sights, custom Pachmayr grips, and strategically placed skateboard tape to reduce hand slippage when I gripped the weapon.

On the back of my body armor carrier, I secured a ten-minute tank of compressed air. The black rubber hose that was attached to the tank valve snaked its way up and over my left shoulder where it attached to my gas mask. The mask would remain draped and hanging under my left arm in the event I needed to don it. Strategically placed "keepers," sewn to the body armor carrier, kept the hose in place over my shoulder.

Strapped to my left side, also under my arm, were my Gerber assault knife and a Leatherman tool. Located just adjacent to my knife was the push-to-talk control for my Saber radio. We were operating in voice privacy to prevent any media interception of our radio traffic.

I picked up my 9mm MP5 submachine gun and inserted a thirty-round magazine of Hydra-Shok ammunition into the magazine well. I slapped the bolt release lever with the palm of my left hand and the bolt fell forward, charging the weapon. I ensured that the selector switch was on safe. I put the canvas harness attached to the frame of the weapon over my head and left shoulder and then let the weapon fall free and hang beneath my left arm.

I walked over and stood by J.D. until the rest of Hotel team gathered around. It was 0255 on day ten of the crisis. The TLs had already independently met with the assault supervisor, and each TL was responsible for updating his respective team with the latest intel. The rest of Hotel team made its way over to J.D. Everyone wore a game face.

With his foot on the seat of a steel folding chair, J.D. looked at each of us for a second, then said, "All right, guys, partner up and do a last minute check of each other's gear. Jump up and down and make sure nothing rattles or falls off." Dave and I did as instructed. This was a common precaution prior to any operation. You always buddy-up and check out each other's gear.

"Okay, there are two suspected hot spots and both are potentially within Hotel team's area of responsibility. The first hot spot is immediately inside and to the right of our initial breach point. The second hot spot is through the lobby and in a room that can only be accessed from inside the cellblock. The floor plan shows a window between hot spot number two and another room off the hallway. We can breach the window and get a 'limited pen' into hot spot number two." Gaining a limited penetration into the room would require that an operator first smash the window with a sledgehammer and then aim the barrel of his weapon into hot spot number two and cover the hostages.

As J.D. explained the location of the hot spots, he pointed to a copy of the Alpha Unit floor plan. The location of the first suspected hot spot would be easy for us to reach; the second would be more difficult. If any inmates tried to get through the door into the room of hotspot number two to harm the hostages, the operator conducting the limited pen would engage the threat. Windows inside jail facilities normally have a wire mesh between multiple panes of glass or Lexan. We would need to remove enough glass or Lexan to allow for the barrel of an MP5.

Simultaneous to the limited pen, other operators would expeditiously move down the hallway into the cellblock, breach the door of the second hot spot, and secure the hostages. The consensus among the negotiators was that the second hot spot was the most likely location of the hostages. This opinion was based upon conversations with the inmates, information provided by the released hostages, and overhears from listening devices, which had successfully been installed or inserted into the facility in conjunction with medical and food deliveries.

This consensus is an example of how the negotiators can assist with tactical planning. Many times during hostage situations, a "Hello" phone is delivered to the hostage takers, which provides two-way communication between the hostage takers and the negotiators. Normally, the phones on each end are connected by one thousand feet of phone cable. As the hostage taker moves around within the crisis site, the negotiators can estimate where the hostage taker is located based upon the amount of line expended inside the crisis site. If the hostage taker allows the hostages to speak on the phone, then the location of the hostages can be estimated. At Talladega, negotiations had occurred face-to-face, and a "Hello" phone was never used.

The location of the second hot spot, which was farther within the interior of the Alpha Unit than the first hot spot, gave the inmates better control of and easier access to the hostages. It also made a rescue by law enforcement more difficult. Saving the hostages from this location would require a flawless breach and unimpeded movement. Precision tactics were fundamental to the success of this mission.

J.D. concluded by saying, "Guys, I've been a member of the HRT since 1983. This is exactly the type of mission the HRT is meant to address. I can't think of a better group of operators to handle this job. Now let's go save nine hostages and kick some inmate ass at the same time." With that, Hotel team headed toward our Suburban. I slid into the driver's seat. J.D. got into the front passenger seat. I barely fit behind the steering wheel with my body armor on. The seat was pushed as far back as it would go. Dave and two other operators climbed into the backseat. The rest of Hotel team stepped up onto the running boards and took hold of the handgrips welded to the body of the Suburban.

The Hotel Suburban was positioned in front of the line of vehicles that, upon the command to move from phase line yellow to phase line green, would slowly taxi across the lawn past the BOP perimeter and stage in front of the Alpha Unit. Tension was high. Everyone was mentally rehearsing his individual responsibilities. We all sat and waited for the command to move. Beads of sweat began to accumulate on my brow. This was a defining moment for *all* HRT operators, past, present, and future. The president of the United States, the attorney general, and the director of the FBI believed that we could successfully rescue the hostages. I reflected on my training. I knew I was ready. It was time.

I watched the rearview mirror and simultaneously ran my hands from one piece of gear attached to my body armor carrier to the next, physically reconfirming I had everything. From my vantage point, everyone seemed to be ready. I heard the radio break squelch. Then I heard the OSC say, "TLs, move from yellow to green. You have compromise authority." J.D. gave me a thumbs-up and said, "Move out, Scar. Take it easy, not too fast." I shifted the transmission into drive and gently pushed the gas, careful not to let my adrenaline surge and cause me to jerk the accelerator with my foot. As the first vehicle in the line of march, my actions would reverberate through the line. I set the pace, and the pace needed to be slow and steady. Remember the adage Smooth is Fast? It's a good rule of thumb in all aspects of the CT business.

As the Hotel Suburban moved forward, each vehicle in the line followed in trace. No headlights or parking lights were in use. All other vehicle lights, to include brake lights and backup lights, were turned off via a switch on the interior dashboard of the vehicles. Ambient starlight and moonlight provided enough light for me to see where I was going. In the event of low visibility or a long distance to travel, infrared (IR) chemical light sticks are attached to the back bumpers of the assault vehicles and the drivers wear night-vision goggles (NVG) with the IR function activated. Each driver can then see the vehicle in front and follow in trace.

The weather was typical for late August in Alabama: the night sky was clear and the air was *moist* and cool. As we approached the BOP perimeter, I could see the shapes of the agents come into focus. They parted and provided a gap for the vehicles to pass through. I looked into the rearview mirror and saw Dave and the other Hotel team operators in the backseat. They were all visibly tense. J.D. was at a "high hover" and the "pucker factor" was way up there. I broke the silence. "Hey guys, just remember: *French toast for breakfast.*" Nerves decompressed within the Suburban.

I looked in the rearview mirror again and Dave and I made eye contact. He had a big, shit-eating grin on his face. I continued to steadily drive the Suburban toward the front of the Alpha Unit. I could see the entry corridor that led to Alpha Six, Hotel team's primary breach point. I lined up the front of the vehicle perpendicular to a point approximately ten yards to the left of Alpha six. As we approached the exterior wall of the building, J.D. couldn't resist saying, "Okay, slow down, Scar." I slowly pulled forward until the front bumper was within inches of the brick wall.

The moment the vehicle came to rest, Hotel team began to dismount from the Suburban. All four doors swung open and we climbed out of the vehicle. Time was of the essence at this point. The inmates could easily detect our presence if they looked out the windows. The radio was quiet. If the inmates were aware of our approach, they would be talking about it, and the sensitive microphones that had been inserted inside the facility would pick up on these conversations. In turn, the CP would let us know via the radio if we had been compromised.

I quickly placed the vehicle in park and turned off the ignition, leaving the keys hanging. This was an SOP. If someone needed to move the vehicle, he didn't have to search for the driver and the keys.

I opened the driver's door and climbed out, quickly moving toward the rear of the vehicle. When I got to the back, I opened the left cargo door. The Hotel breacher met me there and opened the right cargo door. He grabbed the prebuilt explosive charge, and I grabbed the blast shield. All vehicle doors were left ajar so noise was kept to a minimum.

With the blast shield in hand, I headed toward the exterior wall of the Alpha Unit. From where I staged, the rest of Hotel team would fall into line. I leaned the shield against the building, knelt down, and took up the point. My position was just to the rear of an elongated window. This window looked into the first room I was designated to clear upon entry into the facility. The corridor leading to Alpha Six was about ten feet in front of me. I aimed my MP5 toward that opening and held my position.

While I held the point, the rest of Hotel team lined up. Within moments, the breacher would move forward with the exterior door charge. Just as we had rehearsed, the number two man would move forward to provide cover. Still no radio traffic. The number two man passed my right side and headed for the corridor with the Hotel breacher in tow. Number two assumed the point. When he reached the corridor, he made a "quick peek" to see if the area was clear. He then aimed his weapon down the corridor and the breacher moved forward with a pair of bolt cutters. The first task was to cut the padlock and chain that secured the iron gates leading into the corridor. This was accomplished within seconds. The breacher swung the iron gates open and number two stepped into the corridor. The breacher followed and they both moved out of my line of sight. I reassumed the point.

As the Hotel team breacher worked to place the charge on the Alpha Six door, the Golf team breacher was simultaneously working to place their breaching charge on the Alpha Four door. The HRT snipers, who were performing the mission of an assault team, were placing their respective explosive charge on the Alpha Eight door. I didn't realize it at the time, but Murphy was about to step in and make his presence known. Remember Murphy and the adage "If something can go wrong, it will"?

I continued to cover down with my MP5 on the area directly in front of me. I was waiting for the Hotel team breacher and the number two man to reemerge from the corridor. Directly across from my position I could see Echo team hunkered down. They would follow us through the Alpha Six door once it was breached. I could see Nick and Big Jack in their line of march. Big Jack was Echo team's breacher. He was carrying an enormous amount of gear that included a circular saw and a torch. The day before, he was boasting that he weighed 370 pounds with all of his gear and equipment. I believed it. He looked like Freddie Krueger's worst nightmare.

The early morning dew caused condensation to accumulate on the exterior side of the Alpha Unit doors. I could hear conversation over the radio that this moisture was prohibiting the Golf team breacher from securing his explosive charge on the Alpha Four door. The Golf team breacher, better known as Chicken Head, was a Boston native with a thick Boston Irish accent and the temper to go with it. Each breacher carries a spray can of adhesive. Chicken Head sprayed the surface of the door with the adhesive. He placed the rectangular piece of EPIFOAM, which contained the explosive material, up against the door. There was too much moisture. The charge wouldn't adhere to the door. I could picture Chicken Head getting frustrated. Knowing Chicken Head, he would probably opt to stand there and hold the charge in place.

The sniper team breacher was my buddy, Mark. He told me later he was able to get his charge to adhere to the door, but the shock tube got tangled up in the process and he and two other operators were working feverishly to get it untangled. As it was, they didn't have enough shock tube unrolled to get a safe distance from the charge prior to detonation.

Fortunately, the Hotel team breacher was not experiencing the same problems the Golf and sniper team breachers were encountering. The Alpha Six door did not have the accumulation of condensation because it was sheltered within the corridor. The Alpha Four and Alpha Eight doors were exposed directly to the morning dew. The Hotel team breacher set the charge and began to unroll the shock tube. With the number two man providing cover, the two men moved back out of the corridor. They rounded the corner and came into my line of sight. They each passed by my location and rejoined the line of march.

Hotel team hunkered down just adjacent to the exterior cellblock wall of the Alpha Unit. The team conducted the requisite squeeze-back, then J.D. slowly whispered into the small microphone pinned to the front of his body armor carrier, "Hotel at green." Several seconds passed, then each Hotel operator located in the line of march along the exterior wall heard the follow-up response through their individual radio earpieces. "Hotel TL, this is Alpha One. I copy…Hotel at green."

Each assault team then went through the procedure of notifying Alpha One they were at green—phase line green, the last point prior to executing the assault. The time was 0343 hours. Here I was, first in the line of march, point man. I would be the first one through the door. I thought to myself, "No matter what lies ahead, the hostages must be saved."

Life is full of phase lines, some more ominous than others. Years earlier, as I stood over the grave of my brother, I had decided I would make a positive difference. There were no guarantees, but I made the conscious decision to try. Making that decision, no matter what the circumstances, defines life's phase lines. Taking action, based on your decision, is what moves you beyond life's phase lines. Now, in this moment, I knew where I belonged. I'd trained my whole life to get here. I was prepared to save the lives of nine hostages and in return risk mine. I was mentally prepared to shoot and kill without hesitation any inmate who impeded my movement to save the hostages or threatened my life or the life of my teammates.

As I attempted to blade my five-foot-eleven, 210-pound frame in a position behind the blast shield, which would provide protection from the over-pressure from the charge, I noticed two inmates looking out the elongated window directly adjacent to where I was hunkered down. The sensitive listening devices on the inside picked up their conversation. One of the inmates stated, "They're here!" Then the other inmate replied, "Who's here?" They both peered out the window with a look of disbelief and panic. I knew the assault would commence at any moment. It was too late to announce a compromise. I raised a clinched fist to the two inmates, signaling them to hold their position inside the room where they were. The two inmates turned and fled into the cellblock, somehow sensing what was about to happen. They must have realized that if they adhered to my suggestion to stay by the window they would be annihilated when the explosive charge was detonated. My thought had been, "Two less inmates to worry about." My obligation was to save the lives of the hostages, and if two inmates acting as lookouts posed an imminent threat to the hostages, they needed to be neutralized. I could not shoot them with complete accuracy through the thick glass of the jail window; if the explosive charge were to eliminate the threat, then so much the better.

Within seconds, there was radio traffic; Alpha One reaffirmed the assault teams' positions. Then came the command, "This is Alpha One. Stand by...I have control. Five... four...three...two...one...execute!"

At the count of one, the Hotel team breacher fired the shooter he held in his hand. When the primer inside the shooter fired, it ignited the shock tube, which safely separated the breacher and the rest of the line of march from the explosive charge that had been placed on the exterior cellblock doors. On his first attempt, several seconds passed and the charge failed to detonate. The hostages were in imminent danger of being killed! If our breaching charge failed and Golf team and the sniper team were unsuccessful, the inmates would have ample time to kill the hostages. We would be forced to cut our way in with the circular saws the breachers were carrying. Fortunately, this style of shooter has a backup primer just in case a misfire occurs. The breacher recocked the shooter, yelled, "Fire in the hole! Fire in the hole!" and fired again.

This time a thunderous explosion occurred. The over-pressure from the exploding charge, searching for the path of least resistance, rushed out of the entry corridor and spread one hundred and eighty degrees along the exterior wall of the cellblock. With the force of an NFL defensive line rushing in unison to crush the opposing team's quarterback, the over-pressure slammed squarely into my chest, lifting me off the ground and knocking me into a three-hundred-and-sixty-degree-spin. The bailout bottle was ripped loose from the back of my body armor carrier. Designed to provide me with emergency compressed air in a contaminated environment, it now hung suspended from my gas mask hose.

There was no time for repairs. I jumped to my feet and began moving toward the breach point. My 9mm Heckler & Koch MP5 submachine gun was locked and loaded and at the ready gun position as I moved forward into the entry corridor. I knew time was of the essence. The inmates who fled from the window would warn the other inmates of the impending assault, and the hostages would be in extreme danger. As I moved through the entry corridor, I focused straight ahead. Visibility was less than one foot. The seven pounds of explosives utilized in the breach had demolished the corridor walls. Exposed electrical wires hung from the ceiling. A four-foot pile of shattered concrete block lay where the entry doors were located. I switched on the flashlight attached beneath the barrel of my MP5 to increase visibility. The breach had filled the air with suspended dust, and the white light from the flashlight reflected off the dust and decreased visibility even further. "I can't see shit!" I called back to the number two man behind me.

As I maneuvered over the pile of rubble, I probed ahead with my shoulder weapon and yelled, "Get down, get down!"

As I entered the lobby of the Alpha Unit, time seemed to stand still and the events of the moment began to move in slow motion. This is a common occurrence when trying to recall the chronology of a crisis. I was cognizant that the inmates may have blocked our path with desks and miscellaneous furniture. I also anticipated the presence of booby traps, or improvised explosive devices (IEDs), that the inmates may have fashioned and placed in preparation of our assault. I turned ninety degrees to the left and continued to probe ahead with my MP5 as I squared my shoulders and began my movement down the wall of the lobby. I approached the door of the office I was assigned to enter and clear. I moved up to the doorway. This was the room where the two inmates had been looking out the window. The room was demolished. The concrete walls had collapsed inward. Anyone located in this room would have turned into hamburger when the explosive breach detonated.

I reentered the lobby and continued my movement. I relied upon the team rehearsals, my knowledge of the facility floor plan, and my training to navigate forward in the dense dust. I moved to the next office doorway. This was the second room I was responsible to clear. My movement was now based upon the required number of steps I had memorized it would take to reach the back wall of the office. With each pace, I pivoted at the waist and probed with my weapon into the thick suspended dust. I continued to yell, "Get down, get down!" At eleven steps, I reached the back wall. I turned and yelled, "Room clear! Coming out!" I then retraced my steps back into the lobby.

Upon reentering the lobby, I moved quickly and rejoined the Hotel team line of march. I noticed the exterior doors to the Alpha Unit, which we had breached with the initial explosive charge, had been blown, intact, across the lobby and had partially penetrated the opposite cinder block wall into the adjacent hallway. If any inmates were behind those doors or in the lobby when the charge exploded, they were dead meat for sure. The two doors were still locked together, and the inmates, in a feeble attempt to further secure the doors, had fastened the interior door handles together with handcuffs.

I moved into the hallway adjacent to the lobby. There in front of me, prone on the floor, were the two inmates I'd seen through the window. The over-pressure had caught up with them as they tried to run away and had knocked them to the floor. I gave the command, "No se mueva! Don't move or you'll be shot." They lay still on their stomachs with arms and legs spread out.

I heard another explosion. It was one of the other two explosive breaches. The sniper team had delayed their detonation while they continued the attempt to untangle the shock tube. They had notified Alpha One that they were at green despite not having the shock tube untangled. They knew that further delay would increase the chance of compromise and endanger the hostages. They had finally fired the shot and gained entry through Alpha Eight. I found out from Chuck, one of the operators, that the charge was detonated without achieving the proper safe distance via the shock tube. Chuck was the number one man in the line of march. He told me when the charge detonated, two of the operators in the line of march were temporarily knocked unconscious because of their close proximity to the charge. Chuck said when he passed them and heard one of the operators cussing he knew they were okay. The sniper team continued their assault, and the two downed operators were attended to by their team EMT. Chuck went on to say when he entered the cellblock, an inmate aimed a bow and arrow at him. In response, Chuck swung his MP5 submachine gun around and flashed the SureFire flashlight beam at the inmate. The inmate immediately dove onto the linoleum floor and landed in a pile of human feces.

The Golf team explosive charge had not been successful either. The charge had slipped off the door again and failed to breach the Alpha Four door. Upon realizing that the breach had failed to open the door, Chicken Head paused and then yelled, "Go the other way, go the other way!" The command should have been, "Alternate breach!" but the other operators got the message, jumped in line, and followed in trace of Echo team through our breach of the Alpha Six door.

Dave Corderman made his way into the room with the window that provided a view of hot spot number two. The breacher had already broken a hole in the window. Dave poked his MP5 barrel through the window and gained a limited pen. The hostages were in the room. They had stood a mattress on end and placed it up against the door as a barricade. They were leaning against the mattress in an effort to keep the inmates from coming through the door. As Dave held the "limited pen," operators from Charlie team raced through the cellblock en route to the door that the hostages had barricaded. As they reached the door, the Cuban inmates fled. The Charlie team members announced to the hostages that they were coming in. As the first operator entered the room he stated, "Ladies and gentlemen, you've been rescued by the best: the FBI HRT."

Simultaneous to the actions by Hotel and Charlie team, Echo team was securing hot spot number one. They also moved through the lobby and turned right in the hallway. It was there that Big Jack encountered the Cuban inmate ringleader, Jorge Marquez Medina. He was lying on the floor in the fetal position. He had pissed and shit his pants. Medina looked up at Big Jack and muttered, "What haaaappeeeened?" Freddy Krueger would have been proud.

Charlie team quickly made a count of the hostages. Nine hostages were safe and secure inside hot spot number two. This information was passed to the OSC, and the evacuation process began immediately. A hostage corridor was established. In other words, operators lined up so that as the hostages exited they would have safe passage as they made their way out of the Alpha Unit. One-by-one, the hostages were directed to move through the corridor of operators leading to the Alpha Six breach point. From there they were escorted to a hostage holding area where medical staff would conduct a primary medical survey for injuries.

With the hostages secure, J.D. told the members of Hotel team to don their gas masks because of the dense dust and smoke inside the facility. I knelt down and put on my gas mask. With all hostages safe, the rules of engagement changed. Because the threat to the hostages was diminished, if an inmate resisted now, less-than-lethal measures would be employed to gain compliance. The sniper team, which had entered through Alpha Eight, encountered an inmate armed with a slingshot constructed from surgical tubing. He fired half-inch hex nuts at the operators and then fled under a bunk. They quickly remedied his noncompliance. First one and then a second flash-bang were tossed under the bunk. With the second bang, the inmate emerged. Both ears were bleeding from ruptured eardrums. At least he was alive.

As the hostages emerged from hot spot number two and passed through the hostage corridor, I could see in each of their faces the product of malnutrition and sustained terror. Now able to move of their own accord, they shuffled past me in disbelief that the ordeal was over. The shock and the reality of the horrors they had suffered would come later. For now, they were free.

`As the early morning mist` gave way to daylight, the Spartans prepared for conflict. They would face many unknowns on this day, but despite almost-certain death they would succeed. Discipline and courage forged through training would secure victory. Ultimately, innocent lives would be saved.

File No.: Part Three
Subject: Quiet Professionals

In the aftermath of the successful hostage rescue at FCI Talladega, a storm awaited the HRT. Citizen unrest coupled with an increasing distrust in the government would result in missions that would challenge the HRT like never before. This challenge would multiply exponentially with the increased threat radical Islamic terrorists posed.

File No.: Chapter Nine
Subject: Hi Honey, I'm Home!

The FCI Talladega hostage rescue occurred with lightening speed. Despite Murphy's attempt to render the three explosive breaches ineffective, the Hotel team breach succeeded and Hotel team operators reached the hostages within twenty-three seconds after entering the facility through the Alpha Six breach point.

Dave and I remained posted in the hallway as part of the hostage corridor. As soon as the hostages were secured and evacuated from the facility, the FBI SWAT teams along with BOP personnel were given the command to enter and clear the remaining cells. All of the inmates were flex-cuffed, searched for weapons and contraband, and escorted out of the facility where they were turned over to additional BOP officers. Outside, the inmates lay prone on the damp lawn on their stomachs. Their hands remained flex-cuffed behind their backs. Their shoes were removed, and each inmate was subjected to a more thorough search.

Once all of the hostages and inmates were accounted for, the HRT commander directed the HRT to stand down. Upon hearing the command, I made my MP5 safe and let it hang from the harness around my shoulder. Dave did the same. Then we moved back toward the Alpha Six entry point.

As testimony to the expertise and professionalism of the FBI HRT, no shots were fired. No hostages, law enforcement officials, or inmates sustained serious injuries during the rescue. Inmate resistance was minimal. The explosive charges, followed by selective deployment of flash-bangs, stunned the inmates into submission. The basic principles of CQB were successful: speed, surprise, and violence of action. The rehearsals were also invaluable, given the limited visibility caused from the explosive breaches. We overpowered and outgunned the inmates before they could react. Local residents reported that when the assault commenced, the detonation of the explosive charges rocked the entire community of Talladega, Alabama. Not since the War Between the States had the community experienced such an event.

The pile of rubble I had crawled over during the initial entry was gone, cleared away to make access easier. We walked outside and removed our gas masks. It was still dark. FCI Talladega employees and hostage family members were ecstatically yelling and cheering. The BOP and SWAT personnel were high-fiving each other. One of the BOP guards came over to me and gave me a high five. The HRT sniper supervisor, who was standing nearby, immediately turned to one of the HRT TLs and said, "Get the word out. HRT operators *will not* publicly celebrate. We remain quiet professionals." I turned to Dave and said, "That guy needs to loosen up a little." Dave agreed.

The area around us was littered with inmate shoes. As I looked around, I noticed one of the inmates trying to look up from his prone position in the damp grass. A BOP guard immediately said, "Keep your head down and don't move." I turned back to Dave, "Removing the shoes must be meant to keep them from running. Let's go check out the other breach points." We walked over to where the sniper team had made their entry through Alpha Eight. The charge had definitely blown the door. We walked into the cellblock. The condition of the inside was about what I expected. Despite the debris created by the explosive entry, the cellblock was completely destroyed. The inmates had attempted to barricade the door with office desks and chairs, file cabinets, mattresses, anything and everything they could stack in front of the door. Official records and documents were scattered everywhere.

The inmates had dropped numerous edged weapons, which had been constructed from sharpened pieces of metal. They figured out quickly that shank versus MP5 submachine gun is a losing proposition. In addition to shanks were several zip guns, just as I had suspected. Again, a single-round zip gun doesn't fare well against an MP5 with two thirty-round magazines.

Dave and I walked back outside and headed over to the Hotel Suburban where I'd parked it perpendicular to the exterior wall of the Alpha Unit. I couldn't believe my eyes. The vehicle was nearly totaled. I looked over at the Echo team Suburban. It was in the same condition. The side panels of both vehicles were crumpled and the windows were shattered. When the explosive breaches detonated, each Suburban had absorbed the impact of the over-pressure from the charges. The Hotel Suburban was parked between the Hotel and Golf team breach points. The Echo Suburban was parked between the Hotel and sniper team explosive charges. The over-pressure from the charge placed on the Alpha Six door passed through me before it got to the Hotel Suburban. No wonder the Alpha Six explosive charge had knocked me into a 360-degree somersault.

As the HRT began the process of preparing to depart FCI Talladega, a press conference was scheduled at the Department of Justice Building located at Constitution Avenue and 10th Street NW in Washington DC. At 0700 (EDT), Acting U.S. Attorney General William Barr was prepared to deliver comments. Provided below is a summarization of what was said.

ACTING ATTORNEY GENERAL WILLIAM BARR: *Good morning. It's been a long night for many men and women at the*

Department of Justice. I'd like to ask Bill Sessions and Mike Quinlan, Floyd Clarke, and Bill Baker to come up here as well, please.

I have a short statement.

The hostage situation at Talladega is over. At 4:40 a.m., eastern time, I authorized the FBI's Hostage Rescue Team, supported by FBI SWAT teams and Federal Bureau of Prisons' Special Operations Response Teams, to effect a rescue.

I took this step based on the recommendation of the director of the FBI and the director of the Federal Bureau of Prisons that the rescue could be effected with a high probability of success and that further delay would increase the risk to the hostages and others.

All of the hostages were rescued safely, and they are now receiving medical treatment. None were injured in the rescue effort, and no members of the rescue teams were injured. Our preliminary report is that one inmate received a minor injury during the operation.

This was a terrorist incident where the lives of innocent persons were put at risk in an attempt to extort actions by the government. As in any such incident, our concern was minimizing the risk of harm to the hostages and others.

We took action at this time because in our best professional judgment, it was necessary to achieve the goal. We could not make concessions to terrorists holding hostages. To do so would put the thousands of dedicated professionals working in our prisons at constant risk.

Moreover, there was considerable risk that the situation inside the prison would deteriorate, requiring an emergency response. Such an emergency response could increase the risk of harm to the hostages, rescue teams, and inmates.

I would like to thank Mike Quinlan, director of the Federal Bureau of Prisons; William Sessions, director of the FBI; Floyd Clarke, deputy director of the FBI; and Bill Baker, assistant director of criminal investigations at the FBI; and all of the people who worked with them for their superb work throughout the crisis.

But, above all, I would like to express my appreciation to the dedicated law enforcement personnel who took part in this operation. We are grateful beyond words, and proud beyond measure, of their professionalism, dedication to duty, and willingness to put their lives on the line to save the hostages. We truly have the best law enforcement personnel in the world.

I also want to recognize the tremendous resolve of the hostages and their families. They have been put through the most difficult situation imaginable and conducted themselves with courage, honor, and professionalism.

I'd like to ask Bill Sessions if he'd care to make a brief comment.

FBI DIRECTOR WILLIAM SESSIONS: *Thank you, General. The fact that we have been able to come through this very, very difficult time is a mark to the expertise and extremely cooperative effort between the Bureau of Prisons, the Department of Justice, and the FBI. The fact that we were able to come out of this hostage circumstance with no injuries to the hostages, no injuries at all to the hostage rescue team, and only minor injuries to any inmate who was in the prison speaks highly, General, to the professionalism of the law enforcement effort that was made in this connection, and we're proud to be able to have this successful outcome from the effort that was made. Thank you very much.*

BARR: *I'd like to ask Mike Quinlan, the director of the Federal Bureau of Prisons, if he'd care to make a brief comment.*

MICHAEL QUINLAN (DIRECTOR, FEDERAL BUREAU OF PRISONS): *Thank you, General. First of all I would like to thank Acting Attorney General Barr for his tremendous support for this particular initiative to rescue these nine staff members of the Bureau of Prisons and the Immigration and Naturalization Service.*

And I would also like to thank the Federal Bureau of Investigation's Director Sessions, Deputy Director Clarke, and Assistant Director Bill Baker, who have been tremendously supportive here in Washington, and their people down in Talladega, and the staff of the Bureau of Prisons, and the other law enforcement agencies that have worked together so beautifully to have this wonderful result this morning.

I'd also like to express my appreciation to the hostages who have conducted themselves in such a professional way and for their families who have stayed with us and have been supportive during this very difficult time. Thank you.

END OF NEWS CONFERENCE.

The news conference didn't provide any specific details about the assault. From an HRT perspective, this was good. Our job was complete. The hostages were safe. Now it was time for gear maintenance and gear prep then onto the next mission.

At the conclusion of the news conference, Acting AG Barr, Director Quinlan, Director Sessions, and the rest of the FBI executive management team boarded a plane and flew down to FCI Talladega to get a firsthand look at the results of the hostage rescue. Meanwhile the HRT remained preoccupied with the business of ensuring our gear was squared away in the event another crisis occurred somewhere else and we were directed to deploy. In the CT world, the mission at hand always comes to an end, but the job is never over.

J.D. called Hotel team together in front of the jail chapel. He was still at a medium hover, "All right, guys, superb job, but it ain't over yet. We need to do gear maintenance and gear prep. The Four Shop is trying to lock on a plane right now to get us out of here. Each of you knows what needs to be done. We'll toast our success tonight at the hotel over a few beers."

As I walked over to the Hotel Suburban to begin dismantling the ladder system, a woman approached me. She was a relative of one of the hostages. With tears in her eyes, she asked, "Were you one of the officers who helped save the hostages?"

"Yes, ma'am."

She held out a piece of the rubble created by the explosive breach. "Will you sign this for me?"

"I'd be happy to." I took a pen and scribbled my initials and my alpha number, 74, despite the objections the sniper supervisor would probably voice if he found out.

Other than this brief encounter with one of the hostage's relatives and the mere seconds it took to escort the hostages out of the Alpha Unit, I never met, never had any contact with, and never heard anything else about any of the hostages that were rescued. I always considered this odd, but I respected what I presumed to be the hostages' desire for privacy. This void, I also recognized, was part of the dysfunction that exists in the CT world. As an operator, you distance yourself from the hostages prior to the rescue and, inevitably, this distance persists well after the rescue. For the hostages this is probably good. They get on with their lives as best they can. The operators, on the other hand, consume the crisis, and there it remains, rotting in their bellies never to be properly digested.

I reached the Suburban and jumped in the driver's seat, cranked the engine, and maneuvered the vehicle backward through the sea of shoes, rubble, and personnel. The great thing about being within the confines of a penitentiary was that no media and no rubberneckers could disrupt our efforts. I drove the Suburban past the jail chapel and parked near the sally port so I could begin removing the ladders. I spent the next several hours packing up the ladders and surveying the damage to the Hotel Suburban. It would still run and was drivable, but a new Suburban would be ordered upon our return to Quantico. This Suburban would be placed in the inventory of training vehicles.

The next task was maintenance and packing of my personal assault gear, which was blanketed with the fine dust the explosive breach had created. The filter in my gas mask would need to be changed. I wiped down my pistols and my MP5. It was then I noticed that probably the most reliable piece of gear I own was damaged. My Casio G-Shock wristwatch.

I have not received any endorsement from Casio, but when a piece of gear performs exceptionally, it's worth noting. Throughout the CT community, especially within the United States, the Casio G-Shock wristwatch is a signature piece of gear. Durability, dependability, and affordability all contribute to the popularity of the G-Shock. My G-Shock had absorbed the full extent of the over-pressure generated from the initial explosive breach at FCI Talladega, and as a result, the digits that display the time and date were forever realigned in a tilted position.

My G-Shock is testimony to my career as an FBI agent and a CT operator. I purchased the watch in 1986 for around thirty-five dollars. Twenty-one years later, I'm still wearing it and the battery has never been replaced. I've gone through countless watchbands, and I've replaced the ruggedized exterior shell on the body of the watch three times. Since Casio doesn't even manufacture the generation G-Shock I have anymore, the stainless steel watch casing now remains exposed to the elements. It reminds me of Arnold Schwarzenegger in *The Terminator* after all of his cyborg skin was burned away.

My G-Shock survived the assault at Talladega. It persevered despite the rigors of cold weather and coxswain training with the Marines and BUD/S training with the SEALs. In fact, the G-Shock is the watch of choice for underwater navigation, and the SEALs use the G-Shock on their tactical dive boards. Later, my watch continued to perform at Ruby Ridge in Idaho and at the Branch Davidian standoff in Waco, Texas.

During the Waco crisis, I noticed early one morning, as I came off a twenty-four-hour shift in the back of a Bradley Fighting Vehicle, that my G-Shock was no longer on my wrist. I frantically tried to remember where I might have left it. I was scheduled for two Regular Days Off (RDOs), and, unfortunately, wouldn't be back on duty, absent a deliberate assault, for two days. By the time I returned to work, I figured my G-Shock was forever lost.

During my shift, once again sitting inside the back of a Bradley, I decided to have a look around. Uncertain if this was the same Bradley I had been inside two days before, I lowered the back hatch and pulled out all of the seats. No G-Shock. As a last ditch effort, I pulled up the floor panels. I couldn't believe my eyes: there in the hardened steel housing that surrounds the tank tracks, I saw my G-Shock lying there in the grease and grime. I reached down and retrieved my watch. I noticed immediately that the pin connecting the band to the watch was broken. As soon as I saw the tilted digits, I knew for certain that it was mine.

I can't list every mission this G-Shock has endured, but suffice it to say, this G-Shock has traversed the Grand Canyon. It has been with me on operations in Great Britain, Italy, Germany, Poland, Hungary, Japan, Peru, Puerto Rico, Greece, India, and the Middle East. It has deployed with me to Uganda, Nigeria, Kenya, South Africa, Ghana, and Botswana. It has functioned in subzero weather at over 10,000-foot elevations, and in diving conditions of zero visibility, down to 200 feet below sea level. It has been on my wrist while afloat aboard the USS *Belleau Wood* and the USS *Saratoga*. It survived countless HRT selections, thousands of workouts, and tens of thousands of rounds fired downrange.

Throughout all the punishment and all the challenges, my G-Shock has continued to perform. The light function no longer works, and it always runs five minutes fast, which keeps me from being late. I occasionally contemplate buying a new watch, a new generation Casio or maybe something more stylish. I resist this temptation because I know in my heart when I lay down my G-Shock, it will quit running. So I continue to wear it on my wrist every day as a reminder: *Once an operator, always an operator.* I cleaned off the now-tilted face of my G-Shock and finished packing my gear.

Later that morning, the HRT was called together for a brief ceremony on the lawn located in front of the Alpha Unit. Having a ceremony was unusual, but rescuing nine hostages was also something that didn't happen every day. A wooden podium and microphone were placed on the cement walkway. We all gathered in front of the podium with the Alpha Unit to our backs. Acting AG Barr, Director Sessions, HRT Commander Dick Rogers, and an entourage of other officials made their way down the walkway. AG Barr stood behind the podium and addressed the audience. He congratulated us for our efforts, which had led to the successful liberation of the hostages and the resolution of the crisis. Director Sessions then took the mic and echoed Acting AG Barr's comments. ASAC Rogers ceremoniously returned to FCI Talladega Warden Roger Scott a key and the accompanying lock that the inmates had used to secure a chain during the uprising. I turned to Dave and we both agreed it was gratifying to know Acting AG Barr and Director Sessions had the guts to "drop the hammer." It was testimony to their confidence in the HRT.

ASAC Rogers was riding the crest of the wave at this point. He was reaching the time when his command of the HRT would be coming to an end due to the normal two- to three-year rotation. With the success of this mission under his belt, he could write his own ticket regarding his next assignment. Unfortunately, during the next year or so, the wave would come crashing down and, like a receding tidal surge, those in the way would be washed out to sea.

Acting AG Barr would ultimately be named and confirmed as the next U.S. attorney general. His decisiveness and demonstrated ability to make the "hard call" when necessary during the Talladega Hostage Crisis went a long way toward satisfying the Republican administration that he was the best candidate for the job.

After the ceremony with Acting AG Barr, the HRT headed back to the staging area and continued the process of cleaning and packing gear. That afternoon we all convoyed to the hotel. All of our kit bags were packed and our weapons were stowed. Dave and I helped Nick get the white mount-out truck ready for the flight back to Andrews AFB.

The hotel was nothing spectacular. Something along the lines of a roadside Motel 6, but it did have a pool. It was a clear, hot afternoon and the pool became the central point of the post-mission celebration. The trash cans around the pool were filled with ice and cases of beer. Just as the party was getting started, up walked a guy from the U.S. Army Special Forces. I had seen him a few days earlier at the staging area. He was a liaison officer (LNO) whose assignment was to observe how the HRT handled the hostage crisis.

"What's going on?" He walked toward the pool where I was standing.

"It's over," I said. "We conducted the assault and saved the hostages."

"You're kidding! I overslept and missed it."

"Well," I said handing him a beer, "At least you didn't miss the party."

With that, the celebration began. I felt like I was on the football team that had just won the national championship. With one big difference: instead of scoring points, we had saved nine lives and risked ours in the process.

By the side of the pool, J.D. was seated in a chair. Standing up, he asked for everyone's attention. Once all the operators quieted down, J.D. broke the seal on a bottle of whiskey and removed the top. "Gentlemen, a toast." He raised the bottle in the air. "In my hand here, I have a fifth of Jack Daniel's whiskey. You drink it fast, it goes down smooth, and just like the HRT…it will kick your ASS!" J.D. took a long drink from the bottle and then passed it around. The operators let out an enormous yell. The bottle circulated through the ranks…once, before it was empty. When the party finally winded down, not a beer remained. At one point, I watched as Beef tried to shotgun beers while sitting on the bottom of the pool. During the process, he consumed several gallons of pool water. I knew the feeling from pool comp at BUD/S. Later, I heard Beef wasn't feeling too well. I looked around and found him in his room spread eagle on the double bed, snoring like a bear.

The next day began at around 0600. The Four Shop had successfully locked on a C-141 with the Air Force. We mustered in the hotel parking lot by 0630, and were ready to move as a line to the Birmingham International Airport. The Anniston Municipal Airport would not have to worry again about accommodating the large cargo plane. We would go through the same procedure as we had when we prepared to depart Andrews AFB. That had been only eleven days earlier, but it felt like a lifetime. I don't know if there is an explanation for the phenomenon, but ever since I was a wildlands firefighter, it seemed that during a crisis, time slows down. Minutes feel like hours, hours feel like days, and days feel like weeks. Maybe it's because all of your attention and focus is on the matter at hand: accomplishing the mission. The rest of the world is shut out until resolution is achieved, and when you do reemerge, it feels like you've been gone for a long time.

We arrived at the airport and the load masters, including Beef, were ready to begin the process of loading the aircraft. Beef didn't look any worse for wear, in fact he seemed to be energized. We all were. The idea of getting home was enough to transcend the hangovers from the party and fatigue of the previous eleven days. By the end of the day, absent another deployment en route, I would be reunited with my wife and little girl. I had called my wife from the hotel to let her know that everything had gone well. She, like the other HRT wives, had been glued to the television. I explained I would be home soon.

As the mount-out trucks and assault vehicles were being backed up the ramp into the fuselage of the aircraft, I looked across the tarmac at another plane that was loading passengers. This plane was a Boeing 727 bound for Havana, Cuba, and most of the passengers had a one-way ticket. This airlift would transport the Cuban inmates to Havana. At around 0830, they had arrived at Hangar One, east of the main terminal at Birmingham Airport, in two buses.

Security was tight. Dressed in a khaki shirt and pants and wearing tennis shoes, each Cuban inmate wore a belly chain, which attached to handcuffs and leg irons. They shuffled in line from the buses to the stairs that led up to the front fuselage door of the 727. Armed with nightsticks and shotguns, dozens of U.S. Bureau of Prison (BOP) Special Operations Response Team members and U.S. Marshals surrounded the aircraft. There was no chance of these inmates orchestrating another uprising. The BOP did not take kindly to riots within the federal penitentiaries. In fact, the assault to resolve the Talladega uprising was only the second in the BOP's sixty-one-year history. The first one had occurred in 1946 when troops were used to end an uprising at Alcatraz Island near San Francisco, California.

The Cuban inmates faced a grim future. If they were lucky, they would be transported to the Cuban penitentiary Combinado del Este—a facility the United Nations had condemned for human rights violations. Many would possibly never leave the tarmac alive after being turned over to Cuban authorities. After deportation, most of the families of Cuban inmates never heard from them again. It was not uncommon to hear Cuban inmates state that they would rather stay in permanent detention in the U.S. than return to Cuba. The "freedom" they yearned for was not physically in Cuba, but U.S. immigration policies prohibited them from remaining in detention.

At approximately 0900, I watched as the Boeing 727 taxied down the runway and lifted off en route to Havana, Cuba. We, the HRT, had resolved this crisis, but the Cuban inmate dilemma would continue to fester. It remained a ticking time bomb.

The crisis that had erupted at FCI Talladega was, like the aftershocks that accompany an earthquake, a result of the riots that occurred at USP Atlanta and FCI Oakdale in 1987. FCI Talladega would not be the last time the HRT and I would deploy to a jail uprising. In December 2001, another hostage situation would take place in Saint Martinsville, Louisiana.[21] This time the facility was a local jail, but the terrorists were once again federal detainees resisting deportation back to Cuba. The Saint Martinsville hostage crisis was ultimately resolved through negotiations.

By 0930, we were prepared to depart. The flight back to Andrews AFB passed without incident. Most of the operators racked out and slept off the remainder of their hangovers from the previous night's beer bash. When we arrived at Andrews, we deplaned and then boarded a shuttle bus that took us to the terminal. When we were escorted to a conference room, I figured ASAC Rogers wanted to speak to the Team once more while we were together and before we spread in all directions to go home. Director Sessions then walked into the room, welcomed us back home, and expressed his gratitude once more for a job well done. I have great respect for Director William Sessions, and his words meant something to me. Unfortunately, he too would fall victim to upcoming events.

Early that afternoon, I pulled into my neighborhood in Stafford, Virginia, driving the totaled Hotel Suburban. As I pulled into my driveway, my wife came out of the front door holding my little girl. I stepped out of the vehicle and swung the driver's door shut. As it closed, the window fragmented and crashed onto the driveway. My wife looked at the broken glass then at me. I smiled and said, "Hi honey, I'm home!"

File No.: Chapter Ten
Subject: Servare Vitas

On May 5, 1980, when the British 22nd Regiment of the Special Air Service (SAS) successfully assaulted the Iranian Embassy at 16 Princess Gate in London, England, it demonstrated to the world the effectiveness of a highly trained CT team. Six Iranians from the province of Khuzestan had taken control of the Embassy and held twenty-one hostages. Three of the hostages were British citizens. On day six of the crisis, one of the hostages, an Iranian diplomat, was murdered. The SAS mounted an assault. In the end, the SAS commandos shot and killed all the hostage takers but one, Fowzi Badavi Nejad, who was found hiding among the hostages and taken into custody. The hostage takers killed one additional hostage during the assault. The successful resolution of the crisis was a defining moment for the SAS team as well as the entire CT community. The team set a standard that day that challenged all CT teams to strive for similar excellence and success. The FCI Talladega hostage rescue was the HRT's defining moment. Talladega was the HRT's "Princess Gate."

Prior to the FCI Talladega hostage rescue, the HRT was a little known resource that existed behind-the-scenes at large special events and major crises. In recognition of the HRT's efforts at FCI Talladega, the FBI awarded the HRT, as a group, the Medal for Meritorious Achievement. The Medal hangs inside the HRT building at Quantico and includes the names of each operator who participated in the hostage rescue. In addition, each operator was presented with the

U.S. Department of Justice Certificate of Merit, which reads: In recognition of your outstanding performance, courage, and dedication to duty in the counterterrorist tactical support and response to the Talladega Federal Correctional Institution hostage crisis of 1991. Your contribution to the liberation of fellow Department of Justice employees was vital and in the highest tradition of Federal law enforcement. In 1999, years after the Talladega hostage crisis, the FBI awarded an individual Medal for Meritorious Achievement to each HRT operator who participated in the hostage rescue. The medal is inlaid in a wood grained polyhedron sculpture along with a quote from Phillips Brooks that states, "Do not pray for tasks equal to your powers; pray for powers equal to your tasks. Then the doing of your work shall be no miracle, but you shall be a miracle."

In retrospect, the formation of the HRT was not a miracle, but it was visionary and can be contributed to several sources. First, I give enormous credit to the special agents of the Special Operations and Research Unit (SOARU),[22] who recognized the need for a full-time civilian counterterrorist team and subsequently demonstrated the tenacity to create the HRT. Second, I give credit to the first generation operators who set the standard for all generations that have followed. The need for the HRT became evident within its first year of existence.

It was 1984. With the Summer Olympic Games in Los Angeles looming on the horizon and the absence of a civilian counterterrorism team within the United States, Director William Webster was confronted with a dilemma. The United States had not hosted a Summer Olympics since 1932 in Los Angeles. The 1972 Summer Olympics in Munich, Germany, had demonstrated to the world what terrorists were capable of and the debacle that could result if appropriate preparations were not in place. During this crisis, a

Palestinian terrorist organization, known as Black September,[23] ultimately murdered eleven Israeli athletes partially because of a botched rescue attempt by German authorities. No one in Washington DC, or elsewhere, wanted this type of tragedy to occur on his watch, and the 1984 Los Angeles Olympics presented a viable target.

Several years earlier, in 1981, Director Webster had been invited to observe a demonstration hosted by Army Special Forces at Fort Bragg, North Carolina. During the demonstration, Director Webster was confronted with a spectacular display of the Army's ability to conduct a hostage rescue. After the demonstration, the director met the individual operators and noticed that none of them carried handcuffs. When he questioned the Army commandos about the absence of this fundamental piece of law enforcement gear, the response he got was something like, "It's not our job to arrest people." With this question, Director Webster had pointed out the distinct difference between war fighters and law enforcement officers. This also demonstrated why the U.S. military could not be empowered with conducting law enforcement actions within the United States, and these law enforcement actions extended to counterterrorism activities. In addition, the Army commandos nearly had a conniption when it was brought to their attention that they would be required to testify in court about their actions if involved in a crisis that led ultimately to the prosecution of terrorists. This threat combined with what Director Webster had witnessed during the demonstration at Fort Bragg and the vision of the SOARU led to the genesis of the HRT in January 1983. Although the HRT was posted at the Los Angeles Olympics, the Games passed without any serious incident, and use of the Team was not required. Over the next seven years, the HRT deployed to several missions that proved fertile training ground.

In 1985, the still-nascent HRT was deployed to Mountain Home, Arkansas, to deal with an extremist group known as the Covenant, Sword, and Arm of the Lord (CSA).[24] This situation was resolved through negotiation. In 1987, members of the HRT arrested the terrorist Fawaz Yunis[25] in international waters off Cyprus. Yunis had hijacked an airliner at Beirut International Airport in 1985. Still, it was not until the FCI Talladega hostage rescue that the HRT demonstrated to the CT world that it had matured and was capable of conducting a complex, full-Team, dynamic hostage rescue.

On July 4, 1992, almost a year after the success at Talladega, the HRT was deployed to the Grand Canyon in Arizona. I was on another assignment at the time of the deployment and broke off to meet the Team in Arizona. An escaped federal inmate by the name of Danny Ray Horning was terrorizing the national park. Horning had taken some shots at a park ranger and carjacked a vehicle from two British tourists inside the park. The media described Horning as a survivalist with "Rambo" type qualities. He was alleged to have previously placed caches of food and weapons at strategic locations throughout the park.

ASAC Dick Rogers had requested and received an extension from FBIHQ to remain as the commander of the HRT. His success at Talladega had meant he could write his own ticket—and his success continued during the Horning manhunt. Once again, the "ten-day rule" applied, and on day ten of the deployment, Horning was taken into custody. Ten days on the run, for twenty-four hours a day, in the steep terrain of the Grand Canyon was too much to endure; at the time of the arrest, Horning was a physical wreck. Accompanied by HRT operators, professional trackers with their dog teams had stayed after Horning relentlessly. When he was finally captured, he was subjected to the humiliation of having each dog led up to him so the dogs could get a good smell and look at the person they'd been chasing. Horning was returned to federal lockup. I heard several years later that he had been the victim of a jailhouse murder while serving out his sentence. After the Horning capture, the HRT headed back to Quantico. Two political conventions were on the near horizon in preparation for the November 1992 presidential election, and the HRT would be on standby for both. Ultimately, both conventions passed without incident.

Few people could have predicted the dark days to come. The first tragedy was the cold-blooded murder of U.S. Deputy Marshal William Degan. This evolved into a protracted and controversial crisis now known as Ruby Ridge.[26] On August 21, 1992, Deputy Marshal Degan was shot and killed while conducting reconnaissance in preparation to arrest federal fugitive Randy Weaver. Also shot and killed during the initial firefight was Samuel Weaver, Randy Weaver's thirteen-year-old son. Randy Weaver, a Christian Identity follower and a white separatist, barricaded himself and his family in a remote mountain cabin near Ruby Ridge, Idaho. During the siege, Randy Weaver and his accomplice, Kevin Harris, left the cabin and pointed a rifle at an FBI helicopter passing overhead. In response, an HRT sniper shot and wounded Randy Weaver. As Weaver and Harris fled back to the cabin, the HRT sniper fired again at Kevin Harris, critically striking him, but also striking and killing Vicki Weaver, Randy Weaver's wife. Vicki Weaver was holding the cabin door open at the time she was shot, thus aiding and abetting Weaver and Harris as they attempted to seek cover. Once again, the crisis lasted for approximately ten days, but unlike Talladega, this time the standoff was ultimately resolved through negotiation. To date, no one has been held accountable for the murder of Deputy Marshal Degan.

The second tragedy occurred adjacent to the small Central Texas town named Waco. On February 28, 1993, at the Mount Carmel Branch Davidian compound near Waco, Texas, a psychotic religious zealot named Vernon Howell, aka David Koresh,[27] directed the actions that led to the heinous murders of four Bureau of Alcohol, Tobacco, and Firearms (ATF) special agents. Just like Ruby Ridge, the agents, as prescribed within the U.S. Constitution, were in the process of serving and executing federal warrants at the Branch Davidian compound. Their efforts resulted in an ambush by the Davidians and a subsequent gun battle that was unequaled in the annals of American law enforcement. Following the gun battle, a fifty-one-day siege ensued, culminating on April 19, 1993. On this date, during a planned gas insertion by the HRT, the Branch Davidians set fire to their compound and seventy-four Branch Davidians perished in the blaze.

The HRT was deployed to both Ruby Ridge and Waco only to inherit a shit sandwich from other federal agencies. The fallout from the years of scrutiny that followed Ruby Ridge and Waco would end ASAC Rogers's career advancement. Upon the HRT's arrival at both crises, government actions were being heavily scrutinized because loss of life had already occurred. No one could have survived the political fallout destined to happen. The HRT commander was a good scapegoat for the finger pointers at FBIHQ.

The HRT had been applauded for the successful hostage rescue at FCI Talladega, but this changed to criticism and innuendo following Ruby Ridge and Waco. The circumstances at Talladega had clearly delineated who the hostage takers and hostages were. This was ambiguous at both Ruby Ridge and Waco. In both instances, the children were loosely defined as hostages because they had no choice in either matter. As a highly trained counterterrorist team, the

HRT was placed in a paradox in terms of rules of engagement. Since Talladega, a new administration had entered the White House. Ignorance regarding the HRT's capabilities spread from the highest levels of government down to internal management within the FBI. The cabinet-level decision makers who gave the green light at Talladega were gone and those who took their places were inexperienced and indecisive.

This inexperience and indecisiveness would have other ramifications. Concurrent with the tragedy at the Branch Davidian compound, the nation experienced the horror of the first World Trade Center bombing in New York City on February 26, 1993. Despite this demonic effort by radical Islamic terrorists to kill thousands, and the pledge by the bombing's mastermind Ramzi Yousef to strike the World Trade Center again, the United States transgressed into a hallucinogenic stupor, oblivious to the horrors on the horizon.

As the NASDAQ[28] rocketed to new heights, the United States was consumed with the belief that the bubble would never burst. Even the death of 168 Americans on April 19, 1995, in Oklahoma City at the Alfred P. Murrah Federal Building could not shock the nation into the realization that the enemy was within. To add insult to injury, convicted mass murderer Timothy McVeigh stated that his motive for the bombing was retribution for what he believed was the murder of Branch Davidians by U.S. government actions that led to the fire at the Branch Davidian Compound. Again in 1995, Islamic terrorists would strike and kill Americans with a bombing in Saudi Arabia. This was followed by the 1996 Khobar Towers bombing in Saudi Arabia, which killed nineteen and injured two hundred U.S. military personnel. Two hundred and twenty-four more victims perished and four thousand five hundred were injured when two U.S. Embassies in Africa were bombed in 1998. Then in 2000, seventeen more U.S. military personnel lost their lives when the USS *Cole* was bombed in the Port of Yemen. The United States remained unprovoked. What would it take? For eight years, the HRT had languished without a significant deployment. Operators came on the Team and left without ever getting a "call out." The placid attitude of the White House permeated the Department of Justice, where homosexual rights outweighed national security issues. Within the FBI, the consensus inside the beltway was, "Islamic terrorists will never strike in the United States. This is where they raise their money. They won't disrupt this arrangement and bite the hand that feeds them." This denial coupled with U.S. Attorney General Guidelines and internal FBI Intelligence Oversight Board restrictions made investigating potential terrorists, both within and outside the United States, virtually impossible.

To make matters worse, the dynamics of the FBI provided an environment in which terrorism was allowed to flourish. The FBI remained in a reactive posture. This is the investigative strategy ingrained within the FBI and works well when the crime involves a bank robbery, a fugitive, or a kidnapping. These "general criminal" violations fall under the responsibility of the Criminal Investigative Division (CID), historically the bread and butter of the FBI. At the time, terrorism investigations predominately belonged to the National Security Division (NSD) and were addressed by special agents who normally worked foreign counterintelligence (FCI) matters. FCI agents almost never participate in a criminal investigation. Their strategy is to identify and monitor potential spies operating within the United States on behalf of a foreign government. Rarely is a criminal charge of espionage pursued. The United States was at the mercy of the terrorists.

The objective of the terrorists came to fruition on September 11, 2001, when four separate commercial airliners were hijacked and flown like missiles into the World Trade Center and the Pentagon. One of the aircraft went down in rural Pennsylvania due to the courageous passengers who overpowered and thwarted the Islamic terrorists who had another landmark in mind. In all, approximately three thousand Americans died on this day.

With the 2000 presidential election had come a new administration that was immediately confronted with the horrors of September 11, 2001. From the carnage emerged a resolve by President George W. Bush to win the War on Terrorism, a president who was quoted as saying, "Either you're with us or against us." This type of blunt ultimatum is offensive to the squeamish, but it's as American as country music. When attacked, President Bush retaliated. Not with one or two misguided cruise missiles, but with a degree of retribution that was long overdue. The United States was, and remains today, at war with an extremist ideology that is not going away any time soon. This enemy threatens our very existence and is psychologically committed to the demise of Western civilization.

Throughout the mid-nineties, I sat idle with the rest of the HRT. I was approaching six years on the Team, twice the required commitment. In September 1996, I left the HRT and was promoted to FBIHQ as a supervisory special agent. I was assigned to the Domestic Terrorism Counterterrorism Planning Section. I was tasked with responsibilities that would become critical, in terms of national security, over the next few years. I was in charge of the development and management of all Joint Terrorism Task Forces (JTTF) nationwide. At the time, there were only twelve. I recognized the immediate need to have such a resource in every one of the fifty-six FBI field offices. So I began the tedious process of first identifying which field offices might agree to sponsor such an initiative, and then fighting the administrative battle to acquire the requisite funding to support each new JTTF. During my twenty-eight-month tenure at FBIHQ, I increased the number of active JTTFs to eighteen. Soon after the 9/11 attacks, FBIHQ came to the conclusion that every FBI field division should have a JTTF.

In November 1998, I was assigned a new challenge. I was transferred to the New Orleans Field Division and tasked with developing and supervising a brand-new National Infrastructure Protection Computer Intrusion Program (NIPCIP) Squad. This was a long way from my days as an HRT operator, but computer crime investigations were on the rise and this squad was one of the first of its kind. I accepted the challenge with the same mind-set and intent to succeed that I had maintained prior to entering the breach point at FCI Talladega.

The New Orleans Division, not unlike the Louisiana swamplands surrounding the city, was a quagmire of stagnation. The field division was on the ropes due to the lack of any counterterrorism initiatives. While in charge of the JTTF program at FBIHQ, New Orleans was one of the field divisions I contacted to inquire about starting a JTTF. The New Orleans Division had declined the offer.

After one year in the division, I felt the NIPCIP Squad was staffed, equipped, and trained. I was ready to get back into the CT business. I went to the front office and explained that the division was significantly lacking in numerous CT areas that would ultimately become an issue when the New Orleans Division came under inspection in January 2000. This got the attention of executive management. They asked me to elaborate. I explained that the division lacked a viable counterterrorism program: There was no viable special agent bomb technician initiative, no weapons of mass destruction initiative, no aviation security initiative, no capability to address a hazardous materials (HAZMAT) crime scene, and no special events management initiative. There were no viable ongoing counterterrorism investigations, and the intelligence base was nil. I knew that one of the 1993 World Trade Center coconspirators had lived and been educated in southern Louisiana. In addition, the New Orleans Division SWAT team needed an overhaul.

When executive management asked for my recommendation, I suggested that I be allowed to develop a Louisiana-based Joint Terrorism Task Force. This time they agreed and also asked me to spearhead the initiatives that were lacking as well as assume management of the SWAT team. In June 2000, the Louisiana JTTF became official.

On the morning of September 11, 2001, I was pulling into the garage of the New Orleans Field Office when my cell phone rang. It was my wife calling to tell me that the World Trade Center in New York City was under attack. I raced upstairs to my office and turned on the television in time to see another aircraft collide into the second Tower. Within hours, I was contacted by FBIHQ and instructed to deploy to Washington DC. I was one of a select number of CT field supervisors deployed to FBIHQ to take part in the 9/11 investigation. The world was forever changed.

My responsibilities in New Orleans did not end, and I returned there to oversee counterterrorism planning and crisis response associated with the 2002 Super Bowl. This would be the first major event to be held after the 9/11 attacks. With an estimated viewing audience of two billion people worldwide, the Super Bowl was considered an alternative target for a terrorist attack given the amount of resources pledged to the Winter Olympic Games in Salt Lake City, Utah. Super Bowl XXXVI occurred without incident on February 3, 2002. The XIX Olympic Winter Games came and went between the dates of February 8 and February 24, 2002 and also passed without incident.

The ramifications of the 9/11 tragedy would begin to change the long-established attitudes that existed internally within the FBI. The changes would be excruciatingly slow in coming, but just like the final realization that a JTTF was needed in each field division, increased concern began to mount regarding potential terrorist attacks at large special events. The next event looming on the horizon, which provided the greatest cause for concern, was the 2004 Summer Olympic Games in Athens, Greece. I was subsequently assigned as the FBI Olympic coordinator in Athens, Greece. Designated as an international special event, FBIHQ was initially resistant to dedicating resources to it despite the estimated attendance by as many as 250,000 Americans. The proximity of Athens to the Middle East, the historical presence of indigenous as well as transnational terrorists, and the potential availability of soft targets within Greece were all cause for concern. Ultimately, I orchestrated the largest predeployment of FBI resources in history to an overseas special event. The Olympic Games came and went without incident. The mission-oriented mind-set I cultivated while assigned to the HRT and demonstrated at the FCI Talladega Hostage Rescue once again proved invaluable.

I have worked very hard during my FBI career to uphold the law and to do what is morally right. In so doing I have risked my life on numerous occasions. When asked to be the first one through the door at the FCI Talladega hostage rescue, I went. Nine hostages were saved. When an emergency assault option was prestaged to enter the residence of Randy Weaver in Ruby Ridge, Idaho, I was the first in the line of march. When a Branch Davidian reentered the burning conflagration at Waco, I left my Bradley Fighting Vehicle, entered the burning building while receiving sporadic gunfire and carried her to safety. I have testified in federal court and before the United States Congress in defense of the FBI, and helped save the agency $675 million in potential wrongful death damages. I am the recipient of the FBI Medal for Meritorious Achievement, the U.S. Attorney General's Certificate of Merit, the FBI Shield of Bravery, the FBI Medal of Valor, the Federal Law Enforcement Officer's Medal of Valor, and the Attorney General's Award for Exceptional Heroism. When the dust clears, I'll be standing. I take my job seriously.

As I write this, the FBI is fully engaged in the War on Terrorism. It is my hope that the actions of the heroic passengers aboard United Flight 93, who prevented the most heinous crime in American history from becoming even more horrific, will serve as the wake-up call America so desperately needs.

Subject: Epilogue

"Jim, what is your official bureau name?" asked Dr. Nora Davies. Dr. Davies is an industrial psychologist. Renowned in her field and, until recently, on the FBI's payroll, her inquiry about my official bureau name was routine.

"James A. McGee," I responded.

"How about your EOD?"

"I entered on duty on November 17, 1986, Dr. Davies."

"Jim, based on our recent conversations and a review of your work history as well as your personal life, my diagnosis is that you meet the textbook definition of a person suffering from PTSD."

"PTSD! You mean the postwar trauma suffered by war vets?"

"Yes," she answered, "that's exactly what I'm referring to."

She should know. Her expertise in diagnosing and treating Post Traumatic Stress Disorder[29] was well-known. She had already authored several articles about the disorder, and she was completing a book in which she described numerous case studies as well as proposed a treatment that could relieve the effects of the trauma within one face-to-face session. Her efforts in this area led to her leaving the Employee Assistance Program of the FBI and pursuing her own practice. As she related to me, "The FBI was not interested in my efforts to treat and help people, they just wanted me to make referrals."

I respected Dr. Davies and her diagnosis. I personally knew of several other agents who had confided in her. The word was she could be trusted. Having trust was fundamental. The bureau is not a tolerant agency, and attending a session with a shrink could be a career killer.

My interest in talking to Dr. Davies stemmed from an article I read, which she authored, about the trauma associated with grief. My father had recently died unexpectedly from heart failure, and I was interested in talking to her about the stages of grief she had outlined in her article.

"Jim, I understand you also lost your grandfather to a sudden heart attack, and in 1980 your only brother tragically died in an industrial accident."

"That's correct, Dr. Davies," I responded. "My grandfather was in his early seventies, so his loss did not come as a complete surprise. My brother, on the other hand, was only eighteen years old. His death and the events surrounding it continue to be a mystery. I deal with his loss every day of my life."

"I also see you spent six years with the FBI's Hostage Rescue Team. I've conducted sessions with several current and former Team members. I've got to say, Jim, it seems like everyone associated with the HRT either suffers from or is a candidate for PTSD."

It was April 2002 and going on six years since I had left the HRT, but I wasn't going to argue with her about that observation. My knowledge of the symptoms associated with PTSD was rudimentary at best, but I did know that the world of elite counterterrorist teams demanded maximum effort with no room for error. That was the nature of the beast. I knew this type of commitment not only attracted, but also tended to breed dysfunction. Continual training to respond to the worst-case scenario, and then responding and experiencing the trauma associated with this type of critical incident, wreaks havoc on personal relationships and the ability to interact in normal settings. In 1993, when the HRT returned after fifty-one days at Waco, Texas, and the tragedy associated with the Branch Davidian Compound, nothing was immediately offered to the operators. Not that any of the Team members would have displayed the perceived weakness that goes with discussing personal feelings, but there were those who needed help dealing with the fiery deaths that had occurred on that final day.

It was former and current HRT operators who had told me that Dr. Davies could be trusted. Several had even completed the session with her that was meant to release the trauma associated with their own PTSD. The review was mixed regarding the success rate of her treatment.

Dr. Davies continued to describe the origins of PTSD and the positive attributes of her treatment plan. Her phone rang and she excused herself from the room for a moment while she answered the call. During her absence, I reflected on the events of my own life.

My baptism to traumatic events had been a baptism by fire, literally. The job of a United States Forest Service (USFS) wildlands firefighter is one of the most physically demanding and dangerous professions in existence. I thought about the 120 plus fires I responded to over a six-year period as a Helishot and Hotshot for the USFS. I recalled graphically the extreme heat emanating from a Southern California brush fire, prevented from burning as a part of the Smokey the Bear campaign, and then released to consume sixty years of chaparral undergrowth. The requisite heat from the conflagration was so intense that eyebrows were singed and inhaling the thick smoke made breathing difficult. I remembered how my legs burned with fatigue as I ran for my life from approaching walls of flames exceeding ninety feet in height. I recalled watching a converted C-119 slurry bomber, dive-bombing into a fire-consumed canyon. With erratic winds and limited visibility, I watched as the bomber clipped the top of a stand of ponderosa pines. I mourned the loss of the two pilots as the behemoth aircraft tilted and then slowly began a cartwheel descent parallel to the canyon's topography. What had been a 100-acre fire was now a 1000-acre fire, and the remains of the pilots would have to wait to be located and secured until they could be safely extracted the next day.

My mind continued to race. I remembered my experiences as a Deputy Sheriff with the Ventura County Sheriff's Office in Ventura, California. I recalled numerous "accidents with injuries" while working the 101 Freeway. I remembered the suicide calls, the domestic disputes, the homicides, the shootings, the rapes, the broken lives and broken homes resulting from excessive alcohol and drug abuse.

I then reflected on my FBI career. Waco came to mind first and the associated horrors experienced both during the siege and in retrospect. I had spent fifty-one days there in an effort to bring David Koresh and the other Branch Davidians to justice after the brutal murders of four Bureau of Alcohol, Tobacco, and Firearms (ATF) special agents who were attempting to serve federal search and arrest warrants at the Branch Davidian compound. I recalled the events of day fifty-one: April 19, 1993. I remembered watching as the compound erupted into flames on that windswept day. I thought about the horror the flames would bring as they reached the children being held inside the compound. I saw a disoriented woman emerge from the burning structure. Then, in resolute manner, she reentered the fiery tomb. I left my Bradley Fighting Vehicle and, while receiving sporadic gunfire, entered the building to retrieve her. There she was, lying on the floor, prepared to die. I grabbed her, asking, "Where are the children?" She wouldn't reply. The building was coming down around us. The entire structure would collapse within seconds. I carried her to safety.

As the fire diminished, I waded through smoldering embers and charred human remains in an effort to locate any survivors who may have escaped into a subterranean bunker. I entered the center room of the structure. Constructed of eight-inch, reinforced concrete block, this room had not collapsed during the fire. As I entered the room, I descended into the bowels of hell, a hell David Koresh created. Everything in the room glowed like the burning remnants of a campfire. There before me, on the far wall, congregated together, were the remains of over forty individuals: mothers and their children. As I looked around, I realized that the room contained literally millions of rounds of ammunition. The rounds were cooking off as I stood there, shin-deep in bullet casings. Against the wall, still standing upright in their gun racks, were numerous shoulder weapons, all without their wooden gunstocks. I slowly backed out of the room, concerned that my own ammunition and the flash-bangs that hung from my tactical gear would succumb to the heat.

My thoughts then turned to a mountaintop in Idaho, a place called Ruby Ridge. The backcountry of the Idaho panhandle was not completely foreign to me. I had spent several weeks there in 1979 fighting the 100,000-acre Mortar Creek Fire. I contemplated the tragedy surrounding the death of U.S. Deputy Marshal William Degan. I had assisted with extracting the bodies of Samuel and Vickie Weaver. I remembered the long-winded conversations between Randy Weaver and the crisis negotiators. At one point, the on-scene commander (OSC) agreed to allow U.S. Army veteran Colonel Bo Gritz to enter the Weaver structure and attempt to talk Weaver into surrendering. Colonel Gritz was given a code word he was to say out loud in the event he felt his life was in danger. If the distress call came, an HRT emergency assault team was already in position to conduct a rescue. I was the first in the line of march.

The distress call did come and the OSC began the countdown to execute. As I readied myself mentally, I contemplated the route to the breach point. Seven other HRT operators would follow in trace of my movement. I knew Weaver and others in the structure were heavily armed. As the countdown continued, the OSC shouted over the radio, "Abort! Abort!" Apparently, the situation inside the structure defused for the moment. Then, again, the distress call came from inside, and, again, the countdown began, only to be aborted, again. Eventually Colonel Gritz emerged from the cabin unharmed and unaware of the eight HRT operators who were in position and prepared to risk their lives to save his.

As my mind continued to race through various events of my life, Dr. Davies came back into the room. I heard her say, "Jim, given the various traumatic events you've faced, I would like to include you as a case study in my ongoing research regarding PTSD. Would you be willing to assist me?"

I thought about her request for a minute and then replied, "Sure, Doc."

As my conversation with Dr. Davies ended, I appreciated her efforts to extend a hand to help and to understand the mental demons that manifest through trauma. More importantly, she was trying to remove the mental anguish, the undeserved guilt, and the resulting chaos.

In some strange way, she stood at the breach point between control and chaos, between sanity and insanity. Her efforts were analogous to the assault team that received compromise authority and permission to proceed to the point of entry at a crisis site. Whether the breach point—the last location before executing controlled chaos—refers to PTSD or hostage rescue, upon execution, both scenarios require that the obstacles be recognized, confronted, and addressed. Only then can control or sanity be restored. The assault team addresses obstacles via the fundamentals of close quarter battle

(CQB): speed, surprise, and violence of action. For those addressing mental anguish, the obstacles are addressed via self-reflection, courage, and faith. Within the community of counterterrorism, this breach point—the point of no return—has a name: *phase line green*.

Subject: Author's Note

On May 10, 2007, my good friend Don Zembiec called me with devastating news about his youngest son, Douglas. Doug, whom I had known since my time in the Albuquerque office of the FBI, had been killed in Iraq.

Doug, who was serving as a Major in the United States Marine Corps, had completed multiple tours in Iraq and Afghanistan and was in Iraq for the fourth time. Douglas was a man of deep conviction and courage. He was also a man of reflection. While he was home between tours in March 2007, Doug and I had spoken about the war in Iraq. The essence of what he said goes as follows: The United States of America, as well as all free societies, is presently threatened by a radical ideology manifested in the form of fundamentalist Islamic fascism. This threat is nourished by ignorance and desperation, and it multiplies exponentially in the face of complacency. If left unabated, this threat will infest every corner of the world.

Doug knew that the war in Iraq was the stage where the struggle between free societies and Islamic fascism would take shape. He also knew and understood that while his actions were intended to liberate the Iraqi people, a greater goal of protecting and securing the sanctity of free societies all around the globe was his true mission.

If you live in a nation where your rights are protected, Doug was your protector. He did this willingly without hesitation. He did this without your gratitude. What Douglas did want was your support.

Doug returned to Iraq four times, most notably, during 2004, as the captain commanding Echo Company of Battalion 2/1 during

Operation Vigilant Resolve. He knew that the battle remained unfinished and his rightful place was combating those forces that threaten America's freedom. Doug sacrificed his life and left his wife, Pam; one-year-old daughter, Fallyn; parents; and brother to grieve over his grave.

For the United States to do anything less than avenge the death of Major Douglas Zembiec and all those who died before and after at the hands of radical Islam is in direct conflict with their paying the ultimate sacrifice in an effort to preserve our freedom.

Doug Zembiec was the greatest patriot I've ever known. He was a best friend, a confidant, a son to my wife and me, and a brother to my daughters. His death leaves a void in my heart. Doug lived by a simple doctrine, "Be a man of principle. Fight for what you believe in. Keep your word. Live with integrity. Be brave. Believe in something bigger than yourself. Serve your country. Teach. Mentor. Give something back to society. Lead from the front. Conquer your fears. Be a good friend. Be humble, but be self-confident. Appreciate your friends and family. Be a leader and not a follower. Be valorous on the field of battle, and take responsibility for your actions."

On September 29, 2007, I retired from the FBI with nearly twenty-one years of service. Now a faculty member at a major university, I am conducting research on safety and security measures for our university campuses.

My G-Shock quit operating one week after my retirement.

—James A. McGee

Subject: Acknowledgments

Family, Faith, and Fitness, in this order of priority, have been and continue to be the cornerstones of my life. Without the love and support of my wife, Shawna, and my four girls, Shannon, Cory, Devin, and Regen, life's pieces would never come together. I would also like to thank my mother for her guidance, encouragement, patience, and understanding. Mom, you've endured so much, yet through you, I learned nothing is impossible.

Most of what appears between the covers of this text is based upon my personal recollections and experiences. Nevertheless, I could not have completed this project without the help of numerous individuals. I would like to express my gratitude to all of those who have contributed directly or indirectly as my mentors, my motivation and my teammates.

I would like to thank my good friend Dr. Dave Corderman. He is the essence of what it takes to be a counterterrorism operator. I would also like to thank my good friend Don Zembiec, the essence of what it takes to be an FBI Special Agent.

I would like to express my gratitude to Andrew Lenchewski for believing in this project, and for providing invaluable insight and recommendations from the beginning. His encouragement and suggestions were instrumental in making my dream a reality.

I would like to thank my editor, Lianna Wlasiuk. Her expertise was a godsend that brought clarity and chronology to the manuscript. I would also like to thank the folks at Moorsgate Press, specifically Rachel Fichter, senior editor, and Bobby Dawson, who provided the cover design. Their efforts put the finishing touches on a long-awaited final product.

I would like to thank my father. Though he suddenly died when this project was in its infancy, he knew my plan and provided guidance and encouragement. With his passing, the United States lost a hero whose deeds are known only to a few.

Lastly, I would like to thank my little brother, John Kirk McGee. With your passing so many years ago, you took the reins, blazed the trail, and showed me the way. We will all be together again one day on the other side of the river.

Subject: Endnotes

PART ONE

Chapter 1

1. A Special Enforcement Detail is a designated unit within the Ventura County Sheriff's Office that consists of plainclothes deputies assigned to patrol in unmarked vehicles within the county. On many occasions, because the deputies assigned to this unit are dressed in civilian clothing and are driving unmarked vehicles, they personally witness criminal activity.

2. RESMUR stands for Reservation Murders and is the code name for the FBI investigation involving the assassination murder of FBI Special Agents Jack Coler and Ron Williams in June 1975 at the Pine Ridge Indian Reservation in South Dakota. The two agents were ambushed and murdered while investigating the murder of an Indian rights activist named Jeanette Bisonette. Ultimately, the investigation led to the arrest and conviction of an American Indian Movement activist named Leonard Peltier. Pelteir was sentenced to two life terms in jail. Every few years, Peltier becomes eligible for a parole hearing. Each time, numerous liberal "Hollywood" personalities rally to petition for Peltier's release. To date, efforts by dedicated federal, state, and local law enforcement officers have prevented the release of this convicted murderer.

Chapter 2

3. The abbreviation for Composition Four, C-4 Plastic Explosives are a high impact, flexible, adhesive, high quality, very high velocity, military plastic explosive which can be molded to form a shape charge.

4. Non-Electric (NONEL) shock tube is a small diameter, three-layer, plastic tube, which is coated with a reactive explosive compound on its inner wall. When initiated, it propagates a low-energy signal at 6,500 feet per second along the length of the tube.

5. Compromise authority is permission granted to counterterrorism team members to engage hostile targets, thus initiating an assault, while moving from phase line yellow to phase line green.

6. Close Quarter Battle (CQB) refers to the internal room-clearing tactics associated with the movement of an assault force during a hostage rescue. The success of this principle is dependent upon the elements of speed, surprise, and violence of action.

7. The Stockholm Syndrome originated on August 23, 1973, when three women and one man were taken hostage inside a bank in Stockholm, Sweden. Two bank robbers held the hostages for six days. During the crisis, the hostages not only resisted efforts to be rescued, but defended their captors. This bonding between the hostages and hostage takers was determined to be an emotional survival mechanism common during oppressive situations.

8. Also called a "plank owner," a plank holder was an individual who was a crew member of a ship when the ship was placed into commission. The term is not an official Navy term, but it's meaning has been widened to apply to the original members of a group or team. The first generation.

9. An Improvised Explosive Device (IED) is a homemade explosive device consisting of several parts: an initiation system or fuse, explosive fill, a detonator, a power supply for the detonator, and a container.

10. The FBI defines deadly force policy as follows: "Agents may use deadly force only when necessary, that is, when the Agents have probable cause to believe that the subject of such force poses an im-

minent danger of death or serious physical injury to the Agents or other persons. Deadly force may not be used to prevent the escape of a fleeing subject unless there is probable cause to believe that the fleeing suspect poses an imminent danger of death or serious physical injury to the Agents or other persons. Weapons may not be fired solely to disable moving vehicles. If feasible, and if to do so would not increase the danger to the Agents or others, a verbal warning to submit to the authority of the Agent shall be given prior to the use of deadly force." *FBI Manual of Investigative Operations and Guidelines* (MIOG), pt. 2, sec. 12-2.1.

Chapter 3

11. James A. McGee, "A Preliminary Assessment of the Developmental Process Used to Establish Physical Standards for Selection to the Federal Bureau of Investigation's Hostage Rescue Team" (master's thesis, Virginia Commonwealth University, December 1996).

Chapter 4

12. The Rose Valley Flight Crew is a Class I, initial-attack wildland firefighting resource belonging to the United States Forest Service within the Los Padres National Forest, Ojai Ranger District in Ventura County, California. The Rose Valley Flight Crew consisted of a twenty-man Helishot crew, an eight-man Helitack crew, a Bell 212 helicopter with water-dropping and night-flying capabilities with associated pilots and mechanics.

13. OPSEC is the abbreviation for operational security, a fundamental necessity during counterterrorism operations.

PART TWO

Chapter 5

15. The Los Angeles Riots erupted on April 29, 1992. The HRT responded to assist with quelling the disturbance. The rioting crowd was allegedly reacting to the acquittal of the Los Angeles Police Department officers who had been charged with the beating of Rodney King. In reality, many of the rioters had never heard of Rodney King and were utilizing the chaos to loot, pillage, and plunder private businesses. The media inflamed the hysteria by bombarding television and radio with reports that resulted in more violence.

Chapter 6

16. Active listening is a negotiation technique in which the crisis negotiator, while communicating with the subject(s), attempts to defuse intense emotions, return the subject to a normal functioning level, stall the subject, establish rapport and communicate empathy and gain intelligence. Empathy implies objectivity and understanding and thereby builds trust.

17. Third-party intermediary (TPI) is a negotiation technique that is generally avoided unless special interpersonal variables have been assessed as critical to the negotiation process. TPIs are generally requested more so by the subjects than authorities and in many cases escalate the situation and contribute to loss of control for the negotiators. When utilized, TPIs are most successful when under strict control by law enforcement, and when communication with the subject(s) is by telephone. Possible TPIs include psychologist, therapist, lawyer, religious figure, family member, employer, friend, or any other person the subject may wish to communicate with who could possibly defuse the situation.

Chapter 7

18. Attica Correctional Facility is a maximum-security facility located thirty miles south of Buffalo, NY. It is the site of the bloodiest penitentiary riot in U.S. history. During September 9 through 13, 1971, inmates took forty hostages. The final assault by law enforcement authorities resulted in the death of ten hostages and twenty-nine inmates.

Chapter 8

19. Terrorism is defined by the FBI as follows: "The unlawful use of force against persons or property to intimidate or coerce a government, the civilian population, or any segment thereof in the furtherance of political or social objectives." *United States Code of Federal Regulations*, title 28, sec. 0.85 (2007).

20. Mexican Mafia or La eMe (Spanish for the letter *M*) is a notorious California prison gang. Gang member identifiers include tattoos of the letter *M* or the number 13 (*M* is the thirteenth letter in the alphabet).

PART THREE

Chapter 9

21. Saint Martinsville, Louisiana is the location of Saint Martin Parish Jail. During the dates of December 13 to 18, 1999, Cuban inmates overpowered jail officials and held them hostage, including the warden. The crisis was resolved through successful negotiations that allowed the inmates to return to Cuba. All hostages were subsequently released.

Chapter 10

22. The FBI Special Operations and Research Unit (SOARU) consisted of a cadre of special agents with expertise in tactical operations, SWAT training, hostage negotiation, behavioral science, and firearms. Members of the SOARU were responsible for the development of the FBI Hostage Rescue Team. The SOARU has since been absorbed into the FBI's Critical Incident Response Group (CIRG).

23. Black September Organization (BSO) is a Palestinian resistance group founded in 1970. The name Black September is derived from a conflict that began on September 16, 1970, when King Hussein of Jordan declared military rule in response to an attempt by the fedayeen to seize his kingdom. This attempt resulted in the death or expulsion of thousands of Palestinians from Jordan. The BSO began as a small cell of Fatah men determined to take revenge on King Hussein. The BSO is notorious for the kidnap and murder of eleven Israeli athletes and officials during the 1972 Olympic Games in Munich, Germany.

24. Founded in 1971, Covenant, Sword, and Arm of the Lord (CSA) was a paramilitary survivalist group that operated an identity-oriented communal settlement near the Arkansas-Missouri border. Under the guise of being a church, the CSA was a violence-prone purveyor of anti-Semitism and racism. The one hundred-plus inhabitants believed American society was approaching economic collapse, famine, rioting, and a coming war. The CSA stockpiled weapons, ammunition, food, and wilderness survival gear. They trained in the use of weapons in a mock village called Silhouette City.

25. Lebanese skyjacker, Fawaz Yunis, was arrested and imprisoned by the United States. On June 11, 1985, he led a team

of terrorists that hijacked Royal Jordanian Flight 402 with four American nationals aboard. In 1988, Yunis was lured aboard a yacht in international waters off Cyprus, arrested by the FBI, and flown to Andrews Air Force Base. He was the first person charged under the new federal hostage-taking statute that gave the U.S. jurisdiction over terrorist acts overseas involving American citizens. He was sentenced to thirty years incarceration. On February 18, 2005, Yunis was released and deported to Lebanon after serving about half of his sentence.

26. On August 21, 1992, U.S. Deputy Marshal William Degan was murdered at Ruby Ridge, Idaho while participating in a surveillance of federal fugitive Randall Weaver. Deputy Marshall Degan's death occurred during a firefight with Randall Weaver, Samuel Weaver, and Kevin Harris.

27. The leader of a Branch Davidian religious sect, David Koresh believed himself to be the final prophet. A 1993 raid by the U.S. Bureau of Alcohol, Tobacco and Firearms led to a fifty-one day siege. The siege concluded when David Koresh and his followers committed suicide by setting fire to their compound. Seventy-four Branch Davidians died in the blaze.

28. The 1990s were characterized as a decade in which the Dow Jones Industrial Average, the NASDAQ, and the S&P 500 posted the biggest gains in history. According to CNN Money, more than 200 billionaires were created during the 1990s as a result of stock market gains. The 1990s were summarized as the most spectacular market of all time. The Stock Trader's Almanac recorded that more than ten trillion dollars in stock wealth was added between 1994 and 1999.

Epilogue

29. Post Traumatic Stress Disorder (PTSD) is a psychiatric disorder that can occur following the experience of witnessing a life threatening event, military combat, natural disasters, terrorist incidents, serious accidents, or violent personal assaults. Such trauma may result in stress reactions that do not go away and manifest by the person reliving the experience through nightmares, flashbacks, difficulty sleeping, and feeling detached or estranged. The disorder frequently occurs in conjunction with depression, substance abuse, and problems of memory and cognition. The disorder may also result in the person's inability to function in social or family life, including occupational instability, marital problems, family discord, and difficulty in parenting.

Subject: Acronyms

ACL	Anterior Cruciate Ligament
AG	Attorney General
APC	Armored Personnel Carrier
APD	Albuquerque Police Department
ASAC	Assistant Special Agent in Charge
ATF	Alcohol Tobacco and Firearms
ATL	Assistant Team Leader
ATV	All Terrain Vehicle
BJHF	Branch Jail Honor Farm
BOLO	Be On the Look Out
BOP	Bureau of Prisons
BSO	Black September Organization
BUD/S	Basic Underwater Demolition/SEAL
BU-STEED	Bureau Vehicle
C-4	Composition Four
CAT	Counter Assault Team
CCTV	Closed Circuit Television
CID	Criminal Investigative Division
CIRG	Critical Incident Response Group
CONUS	Continental United States
CP	Command Post
CQB	Close Quarter Battle
CS	2-chlorobenzalmalononitrile (Tear Gas)
CSA	Covenant, Arm, and Sword of the Lord
CT	Counterterrorism
CTD	CounterTerrorism Division
DAP	Deliberate Assault Plan

DAV	Disabled American Veteran
D-GA	Democrat-Georgia
DOJ	Department Of Justice
EAP	Emergency Assault Plan
EOD	Enter On Duty
ET	Electronic Technician
ETA	Estimated Time of Arrival
FBIHQ	Federal Bureau of Investigation Headquarters
FCI	Foreign Counter Intelligence
FTX	Field Training Exercise
GEN-7	Generation Seven
G-MAN	Government Man
HAZMAT	Hazardous Material
HBO	High Bureau Officials
HOV	High Occupancy Vehicle
HRT	Hostage Rescue Team
IED	Improvised Explosive Device
INS	Immigration and Naturalization Service
IR	Infrared
JTTF	Joint Terrorism Task Force
La eMe	Mexican Mafia
LZ	Landing Zone
LNO	Liaison Officer
MCMWTC	Marine Corp Mountain Warfare Training Center
MD	Medical Doctor
MRE	Meals Ready to Eat
NVG	Night Vision Goggles
NCIC	National Crime Information Center
NIPCIP	National Infrastructure Protection and Computer Intrusion Program
NONEL	Non-electric
NOTS	New Operator's Training School

NSD	National Security Division
OPORD	Operations Order
OPSEC	Operational Security
OSC	On Scene Commander
PD	Police Department
PT	Physical Training
PTSD	Post Traumatic Stress Disorder
RDO	Regular Day Off
RESMUR	Reservation Murders
SA	Special Agent
SAC	Special Agent in charge
SAS	Special Air Service
SEAL	Sea, Air and Land
SMEAC	Situation, Mission, Execution, Administration, Command and Control
S/O	Sniper/Observer
SOARU	Special Operations And Research Unit
SOP	Standard Operating Procedure
SORT	Special Operations Response Team
SSA	Supervisory Special Agent
S-TOC	Sniper Tactical Operations Center
SWAT	Special Weapons and Tactics
TKO	Technical Knock Out
TL	Team Leader
TOC	Tactical Operations Center
TPI	Third Party Intermediary
UFAC	Unlawful Flight to Avoid Confinement
UFAP	Unlawful Flight to Avoid Prosecution
USFS	United States Forest Service
USP	United States Penitentiary
VCSO	Ventura County Sheriff's Office
WFO	Washington Field Office

Subject: About the Author

James McGee retired from the FBI as one of the most decorated special agents in the bureau's 100-year history. He was awarded the FBI Medal of Merit, the FBI Shield of Bravery, the United States Attorney General's Award for Exceptional Heroism, the Department of Justice Certificate of Merit, the Federal Law Enforcement Officer's Medal of Valor, and the FBI Medal of Valor.

McGee currently lives in Pass Christian, Mississippi, on the Gulf Coast. He works for The Center for Spectator Sport Security Management and teaches graduate classes in Sport Security at The University of Southern Mississippi as well as teaching undergraduate courses in Homeland Security and Terrorism Studies at Tulane University.